Between the Lines

Boyd Cable

Contents

BETWEEN THE LINES

BY

Boyd Cable

FOREWORD

This book, all of which has been written at the Front within sound of the German guns and for the most part within shell and rifle range, is an attempt to tell something of the manner of struggle that has gone on for months between the lines along the Western Front, and more especially of what lies behind and goes to the making of those curt and vague terms in the war communiques. I think that our people at Home will be glad to know more, and ought to know more, of what these bald phrases may actually signify, when, in the other sense, we read 'between the lines.'

Of the people at Home--whom we at the Front have relied upon and looked to more than they may know--many have helped us in heaping measure of deed and thought and thoughtfulness, while others may perhaps have failed somewhat in their full duty, because, as we have been told and re-told to the point of weariness, they 'have not understood' and 'do not realise' and 'were never told.'

If this book brings anything of interest and pleasure to the first, and of understanding to the second, it will very fully have served its double purpose.

> BOYD CABLE.
> 'SOMEWHERE IN FRANCE'
> *Sept.* 15, 1915.

THE ADVANCED TRENCHES

Near Blank, on the Dash-Dot front, a section of advanced trench changed hands several times, finally remaining in our possession.'

For perhaps the twentieth time in half an hour the look-out man in the advanced trench raised his head cautiously over the parapet and peered out into the darkness. A drizzling rain made it almost impossible to see beyond a few yards ahead, but then the German trench was not more than fifty yards off and the space between was criss-crossed and interlaced and a-bristle with the tangle of barb-wire defences erected by both sides. For the twentieth time the look-out peered and twisted his head sideways to listen, and for the twentieth time he was just lowering his head beneath the sheltering parapet when he stopped and stiffened into rigidity. There was no sound apart from the sharp cracks of the rifles near at hand and running diminuendo along the trenches into a rising and falling stutter of reports, the frequent whine and whistle of the more distant bullets, and the quick hiss and 'zipp' of the nearer ones, all sounds so constant and normal that the look-out paid no heed to them, put them, as it were, out of the focus of his hearing, and strained to catch the fainter but far more significant sound of a footstep squelching in the mud, the 'snip' of a wire-cutter at work, the low 'tang' of a jarred wire.

A few hundred yards down the line, a dazzling light sprang out, hung suspended, and slowly floated down, glowing nebulous in the misty rain, and throwing a soft radiance and dusky shadows and gleaming lines of silver along the parapets and wire entanglements.

Intent, the look-out stared to his front for a moment, flung muzzle over the parapet and butt to shoulder, and snapped a quick shot at one of the darker blotches that lay prone beyond the outer tangles of wire. The blotch jerked and sprawled, and the look-out shouted, slipped out the catch of his magazine cut-off, and pumped out the rounds as fast as fingers could work bolt and trigger, the stabbing flashes of the discharge lighting with sharp vivid glares his tense features, set teeth, and scowling eyes. There was a pause and stillness for the space of a couple of quick-drawn breaths, and then--pandemonium!

The forward trench flamed and blazed with spouts of rifle-fire, its slightly curved length clearly defined from end to end by the spitting flashes. Verey lights and magnesium flares turned the darkness to ghastly vivid light, the fierce red and orange of bursting bombs and grenades threw splashes of angry colour on the glistening wet parapets, the flat khaki caps of the British, the dark overcoats of the Germans struggling and hacking in the barb-wires. The eye was confused with the medley of leaping lights and shadows; the ear was dazed with the clamour and up-roar of cracking rifles, screaming bullets, and shattering bombs, the oaths and yells, the shouted orders, the groans and outcries of the wounded. Then from overhead came a savage rush and shriek, a flash of light that showed vivid even amidst the confusion of light, a harder, more vicious crash than all the other crashing reports, and the shrapnel ripped down along the line of the German trench that erupted struggling, hurrying knots of men.

A call from the trench telephone, or the sound of the burst of bomb and rifle fire, had brought the gunners on the jump for their loaded pieces, and once more the guns were taking a hand. Shell after shell roared up overhead and lashed the ground with shrapnel, and for a moment the attack flinched and hung back and swayed uncertainly under the cruel hail. For a moment only, and then it surged on again, seethed and eddied in agitated whirlpools amongst the stakes and strands of the torturing wires, came on again, and with a roar of hate and frenzied triumph leaped at the low parapet. The parapet flamed and roared again in gusts of rapid fire, and the front ranks of the attackers withered and went down in struggling heaps before it. But the ranks behind came on fiercely and poured in over the trench; the lights flickered and danced on plunging bayonets and polished butts; the savage voices of the killing machines were drowned in the more savage clamour of the human fighter, and then . . . comparative silence fell on the trench.

The attack had succeeded, the Germans were in and, save for one little knot of men who had escaped at the last minute, the defenders were killed, wounded, or taken prisoners. The captured trench was shaped like the curve of a tall, thin capital D, a short communication trench leading in to either end from the main firing trench that formed the back of the D and a prolongation outwards from it. The curve was in German hands, but no sooner was this certain than the main trench sprang to angry life. The Germans in the captured curve worked in a desperation of haste, pulling sandbags from what had been the face of the trench and heaving them into place to make a breastwork on the new front, while reinforcements rushed across from the German side and opened fire at the main British trench a score of yards away.

Then, before the gasping takers of the trench could clear the dead and wounded from under their feet, before they could refill their emptied magazines, or settle themselves to new footholds and elbow-rests, the British counter-attack was launched. It was ushered in by a shattering burst of shrapnel. The word had passed to the gunners, careful and minute adjustments had been made, the muzzles had swung round a fraction, and then, suddenly and quick as the men could fling in a round, slam the breech and pull the firing lever, shell after shell had leapt roaring on their way to sweep the trench that had been British, but now was enemy. For ten or fifteen seconds the shrapnel hailed fiercely on the cowering trench; then, at another word down the telephone, the fire shut off abruptly, to re-open almost immediately further forward over the main German trenches.

From the main British trench an officer leaped, another and another heaved themselves over the parapet, and in an instant the long, level edge of the trench was crowded with scrambling, struggling men. With a hoarse yell they flung themselves forward, and the lost trench spouted a whirlwind of fire and lead to meet their rush. But the German defenders had no fair chance of resistance. Their new parapet was not half formed and offered no protection to the stream of bullets that sleeted in on them from rifles and maxims on their flanks. The charging British infantry carried hand grenades and bombs and flung them ahead of them as they ran, and, finally, there was no thicket of barb-wire to check the swing and impetus of the rush. The trench was reached, and again the clamour of voices raised in fear and pain, the hoarse rancour of hate, the shrill agony of death, rose high on the sounds of battle. The rush swept up on the trench, engulfed it as a wave engulfs the cleft on a rock beach, boiled and eddied about it, and then . . . and then . . . swept roaring over it, and on. The counter-attack had succeeded, and the victors were pushing their advantage home in an attack on the main German trench. The remnants of the German defenders were swept back, fighting hopelessly but none the less fiercely. Supports poured out to their assistance, and for a full five minutes the fight raged and swayed in the open between the trenches and among the wire entanglements. The men who fell were trampled, squirming, underfoot in the bloody mire and mud; the fighters stabbed and hacked and struck at short arm-length, fell even to using fists and fingers when the press was too close for weapon play and swing.

But the attack died out at last without the German entanglements being passed or their earthwork being reached. Here and there an odd man had scrambled and torn a way through the wire, only to fall on or before the parapet. Others hung limp or writhing feebly to free themselves from the clutching hooks of the wire. Both sides withdrew, panting and nursing their dripping wounds, to the shelter of their trenches, and both left their dead sprawled in the trampled ooze or stayed to help their wounded crawling painfully back to cover. Immediately the British set about rebuilding their shattered trench and parapet; but before they had well begun the spades had to be flung down again and the rifles snatched to repel another fierce assault. This time a storm of bombs, hand grenades, rifle grenades, and every other fiendish device of high-explosives, preceded the attack. The trench was racked and rent and torn, sections were solidly blown in, and other sections were flung out bodily in yawning crevasses and craters. From end to end the line was wrapped in billowing clouds of reeking smoke, and starred with bursts of fire. The defenders flattened themselves close against the forward parapet that shook and trembled beneath them like a live thing under the rending blasts. The rifles still cracked up and down the line; but, in the main, the soaking, clay-smeared men held still and hung on, grimly waiting and saving their full magazines for the rush they knew would follow. It came at last, and the men breathed a sigh of relief at the escape it meant from the rain of high-explosives. It was their turn now, and the roar of their rifle-fire rang out and the bomb-throwers raised themselves to hurl their carefully-saved missiles on the advancing mass. The mass reeled and split and melted under the fire, but fresh troops were behind and pushing it on, and once more it flooded in on the trench. . . .

Again the British trench had become German, although here and there throughout its length knots of men still fought on, unheeding how the fight had gone elsewhere in the line, and intent solely on their own little circle of slaughter.

But this time the German success was hardly made before it was blotted out. The British supports had been pushed up to the disputed point, and as the remnants of the last defenders straggled back they met the fierce rush of the new and fresh force.

This time it was quicker work. The trench by now was shattered and wrecked out of all real semblance to a defensive work. The edge of the new attack swirled up to it, lipped over and fell bodily into it. For a bare minute the defence fought, but it was overborne and wiped out in that time. The British flung in on top of the defenders like terriers into a rat-pit, and the fighters snarled and worried and scuffled and clutched and tore at each other more like savage brutes than men. The defence was not broken or driven out--it was killed out; and lunging bayonet or smashing butt caught and finished the few that tried to struggle and claw a way out up the slippery trench-sides. Hard on the heels of the victorious attackers came a swarm of men running and staggering to the trench with filled sandbags over their shoulders. As the front of the attack passed on over the wrecked trench and pressed the Germans back across the open, the sandbags were flung down and heaped scientifically in the criss-cross of a fresh breastwork. Other men, laden with coils of wire and stakes and hammers, ran out in front and fell to work erecting a fresh entanglement. In five minutes or ten--for minutes are hard to count and tally at such a time and in such work--the new defence was complete, and the fighters in the open ran back and leapt over into cover.

Once more a steady crackle of rifle-fire ran quivering up and down the line, and from their own trenches the Germans could see, in the light of the flares, a new breastwork facing them, a new entanglement waiting to trap them, a steady stream of fire spitting and sparkling along the line. They could see, too, the heaped dead between the lines, and in their own thinned ranks make some reckoning of the cost of their attempt.

The attempt was over. There were a few score dead lying in ones and twos and little clumped heaps in the black mud; the disputed trench was a reeking shambles of dead and wounded; the turn of the stretcher-bearers and the Red Cross workers had come. There would be another column to add to the Casualty Lists presently, and another bundle of telegrams to be despatched to the 'Next of Kin.'

And to-morrow the official despatch would mention the matter coldly and tersely; and the papers would repeat it; and a million eyes would read with little understanding . . . 'changed hands several times, finally remaining in our possession.'

SHELLS

'...to the right a violent artillery bombardment has been in progress.'--ACTUAL EXTRACT FROM OFFICIAL DESPATCH.

No. 2 Platoon of the Royal Blanks was cooking its breakfast with considerable difficulty and an astonishing amount of cheerfulness when the first shell fell in front of their firing trench. It had rained most of the night, as indeed it had rained most of the past week or the past month. All night long the men had stood on the firing step of the trench, chilled and miserable in their sodden clothing, and sunk in soft sticky mud over the ankles. All night long they had peeped over the parapet, or fired through the loopholes at the German trench a hundred yards off. And all night long they had been galled and stung by that 'desultory rifle fire' that the despatches mention so casually and so often, and that requires to be endured throughout a dragging day and night before its ugliness and unpleasantness can be realised.

No. 2 Platoon had two casualties for the night--a corporal who had paused too long in looking over the parapet while a star-shell flared, and 'caught it' neatly through the forehead, and a private who, in the act of firing through a loop-hole, had been hit by a bullet which glanced off his rifle barrel and completed its resulting ricochet in the private's eyes and head. There were other casualties further along the trench, but outside the immediate ken of No. 2 Platoon, until they were assisted or carried past on their way to the ambulance.

Just after daybreak the desultory fire and the rain together had almost ceased, and No. 2 Platoon set about trying to coax cooking fires out of damp twigs and fragments of biscuit boxes which had been carefully treasured and protected in comparative dryness inside the men's jackets. The breakfast rations consisted of

Army bread--heavy lumps of a doughy elasticity one would think only within the range of badness of a comic paper's 'Mrs. Newlywed'--flint-hard biscuits, cheese, and tea.

'The only complaint against the rations bein' too much plum jam,' said a clay-smeared private, quoting from a much-derided 'Eye-witness' report as he dug out a solid streak of uncooked dough from the centre of his half-loaf and dropped it in the brazier.

Then the first shell landed. It fell some yards outside the parapet, and a column of sooty black smoke shot up and hung heavily in the damp air. No. 2 Platoon treated it lightly.

'Good mornin',' said one man cheerfully, nodding towards the black cloud. 'An' we 'ave not used Pears' soap.'

'Bless me if it ain't our old friend the Coal Box,' said another. 'We 'aven't met one of 'is sort for weeks back.'

'An' here's 'is pal Whistling Willie,' said a third, and they sat listening to the rise-and-fall whistling *s-s-sh-s-s-sh* of a high-angle shell. As the whistle rose to a shriek, the group of men half made a move to duck, but they were too late, and the shell burst with a thunderous bang just short of the front parapet. Mud and lumps of earth splashed and rattled down into the trench, and fragments of iron hurtled singing overhead.

The men cursed angrily. The brazier had been knocked over by a huge clod, half-boiling water was spilt, and, worst of all, the precious dry wood had fallen in the mud and water of the trench bottom. But the men soon had other things than a lost breakfast to think of. A shrapnel crashed overhead and a little to the right, and a sharp scream that died down into deep groans told of the first casualty. Another shell, and then another, roared up and smashed into the soft ground behind the trench, hurting no one, but driving the whole line to crouch low in the narrow pit.

'Get down and lie close everyone,' shouted the young officer of No. 2 Platoon, but the 'crump-crump-crump' of another group of falling shells spoke sterner and more imperative orders than his. For half an hour the big shells fell with systematic and regular precision along the line of the front trench, behind it on the bare ground, and further back towards the supports' trench. The shooting was good, but so were the trenches--deep and narrow, and steep-sided, with dug-outs scooped under the bank and strong traverses localising the effect of any shell that fell exactly on the trench. There were few casualties, and the Royal Blanks were beginning to congratulate themselves on getting off so lightly as the fire slackened and almost died away.

With the rest of the line No. 2 Platoon was painfully moving from its cramped position and trying to stamp and shake the circulation back into its stiffened limbs, when there came a sudden series of swishing rushes and sharp vicious cracks overhead, and ripping thuds of shrapnel across and across the trench. The burst of fire from the light guns was excellently timed. Their high velocity and flat trajectory landed the shells on their mark without any of the whistling rush of approach that marked the bigger shells and gave time to duck into any available cover. The one gust of light shells caught a full dozen men--as many as the half-hour's work of the big guns.

Then the heavies opened again as accurately as before and twice as fast. The trench began to yawn in wide holes, and its sides to crumble and collapse. No. 2 Platoon occupied a portion of the trench that ran out in a blunted angle, and it caught the worst of the fire. One shell falling just short of the front parapet dug a yawning hole and drove in the forward wall of the trench in a tumbled slide of mud and earth. A dug-out and the two men occupying it were completely buried, and the young officer scurried and pushed along to the place shouting for spades. A party fell to work with frantic haste; but all their energy was wasted. The occupants of the buried dug-out were dead when at last the spades found them . . . and broken finger-nails and bleeding finger-tips told a grisly tale of the last desperate struggle for escape and for the breath of life. The officer covered the one convulsed face and starting eyes with his handkerchief, and a private placed a muddy cap over the other.

'Get back to your places and get down,' said the officer quietly, and the men crawled back and crouched low again. For a full hour the line lay under the flail of the big shells that roared and shrieked overhead and thundered crashing along the trenches. For a full hour the men barely moved, except to shift along from a spot where the shaken and crumbling parapet gave insufficient cover from the hailing shrapnel that poured down at intervals, and from the bullets that swept in and smacked venomously into the back of the trench through the shell-rifts in the parapet.

A senior officer made his way slowly along the sodden and quaking trench. He halted beside the young officer and spoke to him a few minutes, asking what the casualties were and hoping vaguely 'they would ease off presently.'

'Can't our own guns do anything?' asked the youngster; 'or won't they let us get out and have a go at them?'

The senior nodded towards the bare stretch of muddy plough before their trench, and the tangle of barbed wire beyond.

'How many men d'you suppose would get there?' he asked.

'Some would,' said the youngster eagerly, 'and anything would be better than sticking here and getting pounded to pieces.'

'We'll see,' said the major moving off. 'They may ask us to try it presently. And if not we'll pull through, I dare say. See that the men keep down, and keep down yourself, Grant. Watch out for a rush through. This may be a preparation for something of the sort.'

He moved along, and the lad flattened himself again against the side of the wet trench.

A word from a man near him turned him round. '. . . a 'tillery Observin' Officer comin'. P'raps our guns are goin' for 'em at last.'

The gunner officer stumbled along the trench towards them. Behind him came his signaller, a coil of wire and a portable telephone in a leather case slung over his shoulder. No. 2 Platoon watched their approach with eager anticipation, and strained ears and attention to catch the conversation that passed between their officer and the artilleryman. And a thrill of disappointment pulsed down the line at the gunner's answer to the first question put to him. 'No,' he said, 'I have orders not to fire unless they come out of the trenches to attack. We'll give 'em gyp if they try it. My guns are laid on their front trench and I can sweep the whole of this front with shrapnel.'

'But why not shut up their guns and put a stop to this?' asked the officer, and his platoon fervently echoed the question in their hearts.

'Not my pidgin,' said the gunner, cautiously peering through the field-glasses he levelled through a convenient loophole. 'That's the Heavies' job. I'm Field, and my guns are too light to say much to these fellows. Look out!' and he stooped low in the trench as the rising rush of sound told of a shell coming down near them.

'That's about an eight-inch,' he said, after the shell had fallen with a crash behind them, a spout of earth and mud leaping up and spattering down over them and fragments singing and whizzing overhead. 'Just tap in on the wire, Jackson, and raise the Battery.'

The telephonist opened his case and lifted out his instrument, groped along the trench wall a few yards and found his wire, joined up to his instruments, dashed off a series of dots and dashes on the 'buzzer,' and spoke into his mouthpiece. No. 2 Platoon watched in fascinated silence and again gave all their attention to listening as the Artillery officer took the receiver.

'. . . That you, Major? . . . Yes, this is Arbuthnot. . . . In the forward firing trench. . . . Yes, pretty lively . . . big stuff they're flinging mostly, and some fourteen-pounder shrap. . . . No, no signs of a move in their trenches. . . . All right, sir, I'll take care. I can't see very well from here, so I'm going to move along a bit. . . . Very well, sir, I'll tap in again higher up. . . . Good-bye.' He handed back the instrument to the telephonist. 'Pack up again,' he said, 'and come along.'

When he had gone No. 2 Platoon turned eagerly on the telephonist, and he ran a gauntlet of anxious questions as he followed the Forward Officer. Nine out of ten of the questions were to the same purpose, and the gunner answered them with some sharpness. He turned angrily at last on one man who put the query in broad Scots accent.

'No,' he said tartly, 'we ain't tryin' to silence their guns. An' if you partickler wants to know why we ain't--well, p'raps them Glasgow townies o' yours can tell you.'

He went on and No. 2 Platoon sank to grim silence. The meaning of the gunner's words were plain enough to all, for had not the papers spoken for weeks back of the Clyde strikes and the shortage of munitions? And the thoughts of all were pithily put in the one sentence by a private of No. 2 Platoon.

'I'd stop cheerful in this blanky 'ell for a week,' he said slowly, 'if so be I 'ad them strikers 'ere alongside me gettin' the same dose.'

All this time there had been a constant although not a heavy rifle fire on the trenches. It had not done much damage, because the Royal Blanks were exposing themselves as little as possible and keeping low down in their narrow trenches. But now the German rifles began to speak faster, and the fire rose to a dull roar. The machine-guns joined in, their sharp rat-tat-tat sounding hard and distinct above the rifles. As the volume of rifle fire increased, so, for a minute, did the shell fire, until the whole line of the Royal Blanks' trenches was vibrating to the crash of the shells and humming with rifle bullets which whizzed overhead or smacked with loud whip-crack reports into the parapet.

The officer of No. 2 Platoon hitched himself higher on the parapet and hoisted a periscope over it. Almost instantly a bullet struck it, shattering the glass to fragments. He lowered it and hastily fitted a new glass, pausing every few moments to bob his head up over the parapet and glance hastily across at the German trench. A second time he raised his instrument to position and in less than a minute it was shot away for a second time.

The Artillery officer came hurrying and stumbling back along the trench, his telephonist labouring behind him. They stopped at the place where they had tapped in before and the telephonist busied himself connecting up his instrument. The Artillery officer flung himself down beside the Platoon commander. 'My confounded wire cut again,' he panted, 'just when I want it too. Sounds as if they meant a rush, eh?' The infantryman nodded. 'Will they stop shelling before they rush?' he shouted.

'Not till their men are well out in front. Their guns can keep going over their heads for a bit. Are you through, Jackson? Tell the Battery to "eyes front." It looks like an attack.'

The telephonist repeated the message, listened a moment and commenced, 'The Major says, sir----' when his officer interrupted sharply, 'Three rounds gun-fire--quick.'

'Three rounds gun-fire--quick, sir,' bellowed the telephonist into his mouthpiece.

'Here they come, lads. Let 'em have it,' yelled the Platoon commander, and commenced himself to fire through a loophole.

At the same moment there came from the rear the quick thudding reports of the British guns, the rush of their shells overhead, and the sharp crash of their shells over the German parapets.

'All fired, sir,' called the telephonist.

'Battery fire one second,' the Observing Officer shouted without turning his head from his watch over the parapet.

'Number one fired--two fired--three fired,' the signaller called rapidly, and the Observing Officer watched narrowly the white cotton-wool clouds of the bursting shrapnel of his guns.

'Number three, ten minutes more right--all guns, drop twenty-five--repeat,' he ordered, and in swift obedience the guns began to drop their shrapnel showers, sweeping along the ground in front of the German trench.

But the expected rush of Germans hung fire. A line of bobbing heads and shoulders had showed above their parapet and only a few scattered groups had clambered over its top.

'They're beat,' shouted the infantry officer, exultingly. 'They're dodging back. Give it to 'em, boys--give it--ow!' He broke off and ducked down with a hand clapped to his cheek where a bullet had scored its way.

'Get down! get down! Make your men get down,' said the gunner officer rapidly. 'It's all . . .'

Again there came the swishing rush of the light shells, a series of quick-following bangs, and a hail of shrapnel tearing across the trench, before the men had time to duck.

'All a false alarm--just a dodge to get your men's heads up within reach of their Fizz-Bangs' shrapnel,' said the artilleryman, and called to the signaller. 'All guns raise twenty-five. Section fire five seconds. . . . Hullo--hit?' he continued to the Platoon officer, as he noticed him wiping a smear of blood from his cheek.

'Just a nice little scratch,' said the lad, grinning. 'Enough to let me swank about being wounded and show off a pretty scar to my best girl when the war's over.'

'Afraid that last shrapnel burst gave some of your fellows more'n a pretty scar,' said the gunner. 'But I suppose I'd better slow my guns up again. . . . Jackson, tell them the attack's evidently stopped--section fire ten seconds.'

'Can't you keep on belting 'em for a bit?' asked the Platoon officer. 'Might make 'em ease up on us.'

The gunner shook his head regretfully.

'I'd ask nothing better,' he said. 'I could just give those trenches beans. But our orders are strict, and we daren't waste a round on anything but an attack. I'll bet that's my Major wanting to know if he can't slack off a bit more,' he continued, as the signaller called something about 'Wanted to speak here, sir.'

He went to the instrument and held a short conversation. 'Told you so,' he said, when he returned to the infantry officer. 'No attack--no shells. We're stopping again.'

'Doesn't seem to be too much stop about the Germs,' grumbled the infantryman, as another series of crackling shells shook the ground close behind them. He moved down the line speaking a few words here and there to the crouching men of his platoon.

'This is getting serious,' he said when he came back to his place. 'There's more than the half of my lot hit, and the most of them pretty badly. These shrapnel bullets and shell splinters make a shocking mess of a wound, y'know.'

'Yes,' said the gunner grimly, 'I know.'

'A perfectly brutal mess,' the subaltern repeated. 'A bullet now is more or less decent, but those shells of theirs, they don't give a man a chance to pull through.'

'Ours are as bad, if that's any satisfaction to you,' said the gunner.

'I s'pose so,' agreed the subaltern. 'Ghastly sort of game altogether, isn't it? Those poor fellows of mine now--the killed, I mean. Think of their fathers and mothers and wives or sweethearts----'

'I'd rather not,' said the gunner. 'And I shouldn't advise you to. Better not to think of these things.'

'I wish they'd come again,' said the Platoon commander. 'It would stop the shells for a bit perhaps. They're getting on my nerves. One's so helpless against them, sticking here waiting to know where the next will drop. And they don't even give a fellow the ordinary four to one chance of a casualty being a wound only. They make such a cruel messy smash of a fellow.... Are you going?'

'Must find that break in my wire,' said the gunner, and presently he and the telephonist ploughed off along the trench.

The bombardment continued with varying intensity throughout the day. There was no grand finale, no spectacular rush or charge, no crashing assault, no heroic hand-to-hand combats--no anything but the long-drawn agony of lying still and being hammered by the crashing shells. This was no 'artillery preparation for the assault,' although the Royal Blanks did not know that and so dare not stir from the danger zone of the forward trench. They were not even to have the satisfaction of giving back some of the punishment they had endured, or the glory--a glory carefully concealed from their friends at home, and mostly lost by the disguising or veiling of their identity in the newspapers, but still a glory--of taking a trench or making a successful attack or counter-attack. It was merely another 'heavy artillery bombardment,' lived through and endured all unknown, as so many have been endured.

The Royal Blanks were relieved at nightfall when the fire had died down. The Artillery Observing Officer was just outside the communication trench at the relief hour and saw the casualties being helped or carried out. A stretcher passed and the figure on it had a muddy and dark-stained blanket spread over, and an officer's cap and binoculars on top.

'An officer?' asked the gunner. 'Who is it?' 'Mr. Grant, sir,' said one of the stretcher-bearers dully. 'No. 2 Platoon.'

The gunner noted the empty sag of the blanket where the head and shoulders should have been outlined and checked the half-formed question of 'Badly hit?' to 'How was it?'

'Shell, sir. A Fizz-Bang hit the parapet just where 'e was lyin'. Caught 'im fair.'

The bearers moved on, leaving the gunner groping in his memory for a sentence in the youngster's last talk he had heard. "Ghastly business . . . cruel messy smash,' he murmured.

'Beg pardon, sir?' said the telephonist.

The Forward Officer made no answer but continued to stare after the disappearing stretcher-bearers. The signaller shuffled his feet in the mud and hitched up the strap of the instrument on his shoulder.

'I suppose it's all over now, sir,' he said.

'Yes, all over--except for his father, or mother, or sweetheart,' said the officer absently.

The signaller stared. 'I meant the shellin', sir.'

'Oh--ah, yes; the shelling, Jackson. Yes, I dare say that's over for to-night, since they seem to have stopped now.'

'P'raps we might see about some food, sir,' said the signaller.

'Food--to be sure,' said the officer briskly. 'Eat, drink, and be merry, Jackson, for--I'm hungry too, now I think of it. And, oh Lord, I'm tired.'

No. 2 Platoon were tired too, as they filed wearily out by the communication trench, tired and worn out mentally and physically--and yet not too tired or too broken for a light word or a jest. From the darkness behind them a German flare soared up and burst, throwing up bushes and shattered buildings, sandbag parapets, broken tree-stumps, sticks and stones in luminous-edged silhouette. A machine-gun burst into a stutter of fire, the reports sounding faint at first and louder and louder as the muzzle swept round in its arc. 'Ssh-sh-sh-sh,' the bullets swept over-head, and No. 2 Platoon halted and crouched low in the shallow communication trench.

'Oh, shut it, blast ye,' growled one of the men disgustedly. 'Ain't we 'ad enough for one day?'

'It's only 'im singin' 'is little evenin' hymn as usual,' said another.

'Just sayin' 'is good-bye an' sendin' a few partin' sooveniers'; and another sang 'Say aw rev-wore, but not good-bye.'

'Stop that howling there,' a sergeant called down the line, 'and stop smoking those cigarettes and talking.'

'Certainly, sergeant,' a voice came back. 'An' please sergeant, will you allow us to keep on breathin'?'

The light died, and the line rose and moved on, squelching softly in the mud. A man clapped a hand to his pocket, half halted and exclaimed in annoyance. 'Blest if I 'aven't left my mouth-organ back there,' he said. 'Hutt!' said his next file. 'Be glad ye've a mouth left, or a head to have a mouth. It might be worse, an' ye might be left back there yerself decoratin' about ten square yards of trench.'

'Tut-tut-tut-tut' went the maxim behind them again.

'Tutt-tutt yourself, you stammer-an'-spit blighter,' said the disconsolate mouth-organ loser, and 'D'you think we can chance a smoke yet?' as the platoon moved out on the road and behind the shelter of some ruined house-walls.

Platoon by platoon the company filed out and formed up roughly behind the houses. The order to move came at last and the ranked fours swung off, tramping slowly and stolidly in silence until some one struck up a song--

'Crump, crump, crump, says the big bustin' shells----

A chorus of protest and a 'Give the shells a rest' stopped the song on the first line, and it was to the old regimental tune, the canteen and sing-song favourite, 'The Sergeant's Return,' that the Royal Blanks settled itself into its pack shoulder-straps and tramped on.

I'm the same ol' feller that you always used to know--   Oh! Oh! you know you used to know-- An' it's years since we parted way down on Plymouth Hoe-- Oh! Oh! So many years ago.   I've roamed around the world, but I've come back to you,   For my 'eart 'as never altered, my 'eart is ever true.   [Prolonged and noisy imitation of a kiss.]   ***Ain't*** that got the taste you always used to know?

The colonel was talking to the adjutant in the road as the companies moved past, and he noted with some concern the ragged ranks and listless movement of the first lot to pass.

'They're looking badly tucked up,' he said.

'They've had a cruel day,' said the adjutant.

'Yes, the worst kind,' agreed the O.C. 'And I doubt if they can stand that sort of thing so well now. The old regiment is not what it used to be. We're so filled up with recruits now--youngsters too. . . . Here's B company--about the rawest of the lot and caught the worst of it to-day. How d'you think they stand it?'

But it was B company that answered the question for itself and the old regiment, singing the answer softly to itself and the O.C. as it trudged past--

I'm the same ol' feller that you always used to know--   Oh! Oh! you know you used to know. . . .

'Gad, Malcolm,' said the O.C. straightening his own shoulders, 'they'll do, they'll do.'

 . . . My 'eart 'as never altered, my 'eart is ever true,

the remnant of No. 2 Platoon sang past him.

'They haven't shaken us yet,' said the O.C. proudly.

'Tutt, tutt!' grumbled the maxim faintly. 'Tutt, tutt!'

THE MINE

'. . . a mine was successfully exploded under a section of the enemy's trench.
. . .'--ACTUAL EXTRACT FROM AN OFFICIAL DESPATCH.

Work on the sap-head had been commenced on what the Captain of the Sappers called 'a beautiful night,' and what anyone else outside a lunatic asylum would have described with the strongest adjectives available in exactly the opposite sense. A piercing wind was blowing in gusts of driving sleet and rain, it was pitch dark--'black as the inside of a cow,' as the Corporal put it--and it was bitterly cold. But, since all these conditions are exactly those most calculated to make difficult the work of an enemy's sentries and look-outs, and the first work of sinking a shaft is one which it is highly desirable should be unobserved by an enemy, the Sapper Captain's satisfaction may be understood.

The sap-head was situated amongst the ruins of a cottage a few yards behind the forward firing trench, and by the time a wet daylight had dawned the Sappers had dug themselves well underground, had securely planked up the walls of the shaft, and had cut a connecting gallery from the ruins to the communication trench. All this meant that their work was fairly free from observation, and the workers reasonably safe from bombs and bullets, so that the officer in charge had good cause for the satisfaction with which he made his first report.

His first part of the work had been a matter of plans and maps, of compass and level, of observing the ground--incidentally dodging the bullets of the German snipers who caught glimpses of his crawling form--by day, and of intricate and exact figuring and calculating by night, in the grimy cellar of another ruined house by the light of a candle, stuck in an empty bottle.

Thereafter he spent all his waking hours (and many of his sleeping ones as well) in a thick suit of clayey mud; he lived like a mole in his mine gallery or his underground cellar, saw the light only when he emerged to pass from his work to his sleep or meals, and back to his work, and generally gave himself, his whole body and brain and being, to the correct driving of a shallow burrow straight to the selected point under the enemy trench a hundred and odd yards away. He was a youngish man, and this was the first job of any importance that had been wholly and solely entrusted to him. It was not only his anxiety to make a creditable showing, but he was keen on the work for the work's own sake, and he revelled in the creative sense of the true artist. The mine was his. He had first suggested it, he had surveyed it, and plotted it, and measured and planned and worked it out on paper; and now, when it came to the actual pick-and-shovel work, he supervised and directed and watched each hour of work, and each yard of progress.

It was tricky work, too, and troublesome. At first the ground was good stiff clay that the spades bit out in clean mouthfuls, and that left a fair firm wall behind. But that streak ran out in the second day's working, and the mine burrowed into some horrible soft crumbly soil that had to be held up and back by roof and wall of planking. The Subaltern took a party himself and looted the wrecks of houses--there was no lack of these in the village just behind the lines--of roof-beams and flooring, and measured and marked them for sawing into lengths, and would have taken a saw with pleasure himself.

Then he dived cheerfully into the oozing wet burrow and superintended the shoring up, and re-started the men to digging, and emerged a moment to see more planking passed down. He came in fact dangerously near to making a nuisance of himself, and some of his men who had been sapping and mining for wet and weary months past were inclined to resent quite so much fussing round and superintendence. But the Corporal put that right. He was an elderly man with a nasty turn of temper that had got him into almost as many troubles in his service as his knowledge, experience, and aptitude for hard work and responsibility had got him out of.

'Leave the lad be,' he had said when some of the party had passed grumbling remarks about 'too bloomin' much fuss an' feathers over a straight simple bloomin' job.' The Corporal had promptly squashed that opinion. 'Leave the lad be,' he said.

'He's young to the job, mebbe, but he's not such a simple fool as some that take this for a simple job. It's not goin' to be all that simple, as you'll find before you're done.'

He was right, too. The crumbling soil was one little difficulty promptly and easily met. The next was more troublesome. The soil grew wetter and more wet until at last the men were working ankle deep in water. The further the mine went the wetter it became. The men worked on, taking their turn at the narrow face, shovelling out the wet muck and dragging it back to the shaft and up and out and away by the communication trench. They squeezed aside in silence when the Sub-altern pushed in to inspect the working, and waited with side winks to one another to see what he would do to overcome the water difficulty. 'Pumps' would of course have been the simple answer, but the men knew as well as the Subaltern knew that pumps were not to be had at that particular time and place for love or money, and that all the filling of all the 'indents' in the R.E. would not produce one single ef-ficient pump from store.

The Subaltern did not trouble with indent forms or stores. He had had some-thing of a fight to get a grudging permission for his mine, and he felt it in his bones that if he worried the big chiefs too much with requisitions he would be told to abandon the mine. He shut his teeth tight at the thought. It was his mine and he was going to see it through, if he had to bale the water out with a tea-cup.

He made a quick cast through the shell-wrecked village, drew blank, sat for fifteen minutes on the curb of a rubble-choked well and thought hard, jumped up and called the Corporal to provide him with four men and some odd tools, and struck back across muddy and shell-cratered fields to the nearest farm. The farmer, who had remained in possession despite the daily proximity of bursting shells, a shrapnel-smashed tile roof, and a gaping hole where one house-corner should have been, made some objection to the commandeering of his old-fashioned farm pump. He was at first supported in this by the officer in charge of the men billeted in the barn and sheds, but the Sapper explained the urgency of his need and cunningly clinched the argument by reminding the Infantry officer that probably he and his men would soon be installed in the trenches from which the mine ran, and that he--the Sapper--although he was not supposed to mention it, might just hint that his mine was only hurrying to forestall an enemy mine which was judged to be ap-

proaching the trench the Infantry officer would presently occupy. This last was a
sheer invention of the moment, but it served excellently, and the Sapper and his
party bore off their pump in triumph. It was later erected in the mine shaft, and the
difficulty of providing sufficient piping to run from the pump to the waterlogged
part of the mine was met by a midnight visit to the house where Headquarters
abode and the wholesale removal of gutters and rain-pipes. As Headquarters had
its principal residence in a commodious and cobwebby cellar, the absence of the
gutters fortunately passed without remark, and the sentry who watched the looting
and the sergeant to whom he reported it were quite satisfied by the presence of an
Engineer officer and his calm assurance that it was 'all right--orders--an Engineers'
job.'

The pump did its work excellently, and a steady stream of muddy water gushed
from its nozzle and flowed down the Headquarters gutter-pipes to a selected spot
well behind the trenches. Unfortunately the pump, being old-fashioned, was somewhat noisy, and all the packing and oiling and tinkering failed to silence its clank-
clink, clank-clink, as its arm rose and fell.

The nearest German trench caught the clank-clink, and by a simple process of
deduction and elimination arrived at its meaning and its location. The pump and
the pumpers led a troubled life after that. Snipers kept an unsteady but never silent
series of bullets smacking into the stones of the ruin, whistling over the communication trench, and 'whupp'-ing into the mud around both. A light gun took a hand
and plumped a number of rounds each day into the crumbling walls and rubbish-
heaps of stone and brick, and burst shrapnel all over the lot. The Sappers dodged
the snipers by keeping tight and close to cover; they frustrated the direct-hitting
'Fizz-Bang' shells by a stout barricade of many thicknesses of sandbags bolstering
up the fragment of wall that hid their shaft and pump, and finally they erected a
low roof over the works and sandbagged that secure against the shrapnel. There
were casualties of course, but these are always in the way of business with the Sappers and came as a matter of course. The Germans brought up a trench-mortar next
and flung noisy and nerve-wrecking high-explosive bombs into and all round the
ruin, bursting down all the remaining walls except the sandbagged one and scoring
a few more casualties until the forward trench installed a trench-mortar of their
own, and by a generous return of two bombs to the enemy's one put the German

out of action. A big *minnenwerfer* came into play next, and because it could throw
a murderous-sized bomb from far behind the German trench it was too much for
the British trench-mortar to tackle. This brought the gunners into the game, and
the harassed infantry (who were coming to look on the Sapper Subaltern and his
works as an unmitigated nuisance and a most undesirable acquaintance who drew
more than a fair share of enemy fire on them) appealed to the guns to rid them of
their latest tormentor. An Artillery Observing Officer spent a perilous hour or two
amongst the shrapnel and snipers' bullets on top of the sandbagged wall, until he
had located the *minnenwerfer*. Then about two minutes' telephoned talk to the
Battery and ten minutes of spouting lyddite volcanoes finished the *minnenwerfer*
trouble. But all this above-ground work was by way of an aside to the Sapper Subaltern. He was far too busy with his mine gallery to worry about the doings of gunners and bomb-throwers and infantry and such-like fellows. When these people
interfered with his work they were a nuisance of course, but he always managed to
find a working party for the sandbagging protective work without stopping the job
underground.

So the gallery crept steadily on. They had to carry the tunnel rather close to
the surface because at very little depth they struck more water than any pumps,
much less their single farmyard one, could cope with. The nearness to the surface made a fresh difficulty and necessitated the greatest care in working under the
ground between the trenches, because here there were always deep shell-holes and
craters to be avoided or floored with the planking that made the tunnel roof. So the
gallery had to be driven carefully at a level below the danger of exposure through
a shell-hole and above the depth at which the water lay. This meant a tunnel too
low to stand or even kneel in with a straight back, and the men, kneeling in mud,
crouched back on their heels and with rounded back and shoulders, struck their
spades forward into the face and dragged the earth out spadeful by spadeful. Despite the numbing cold mud they knelt in, the men, stripped to shirts with rolled
sleeves and open throats, streamed rivulets of sweat as they worked; for the air was
close and thick and heavy, and the exertion in the cramped space was one long
muscle-racking strain.

Once the roof and walls caved in, and three men were imprisoned. The collapse came during the night, fortunately, and, still more fortunately behind the line

and parapet of the forward trench. The Subaltern flung himself and his men on the muddy wreckage in frantic haste to clear an opening and admit air to the imprisoned men. It took time, a heart-breaking length of time; and it was with a horrible dread in his heart that the Subaltern at last pushed in to the uncovered opening and crawled along the tunnel, flashing his electric torch before him. Half-way to the end he felt a draught of cold air, and, promptly extinguishing his lamp, saw a hole in the roof. His men were alive all right, and not only alive but keeping on hard at work at the end of the tunnel. When the collapse came they had gone back to where their roof lay across the bottom of a shell-hole, pulled a plank out, and--gone back to work.

When the tunnel reached a point under the German parapet it was turned sharp to left and right, forming a capital T with the cross-piece running roughly along the line of trench and parapet. Here there was need of the utmost deliberation and caution. A pick could not be used, and even a spade had to be handled gently, in case the sounds of working should reach the Germans overhead. In some places the Subaltern could actually hear the movements and footsteps of the enemy just above him.

Twice the diggers disturbed a dead German, buried evidently under the parapet. Once a significant crumbling of the earth and fall of a few heavy clods threatened a collapse where the gallery was under the edge of the trench. The spot was hastily but securely shored up with infinite caution and the least possible sound, and after that the Subaltern had the explosive charges brought along and connected up in readiness. Then, if the roof collapsed or their work were discovered, the switch at the shaft could still be pressed, the wires would still carry the current, and the mine would be exploded.

At last the Subaltern decided that everything was ready. He carefully placed his charges, connected up his wires again, cleared out his tools, and emerged to report 'all ready.'

Now the 'touching off' of a good-sized mine is not a matter to be done lightly or without due and weighty authority, and that because more is meant to result from it than the upheaval of some square yards of earth and the destruction of so many yards of enemy trench. The mine itself, elaborate and labour-making as it may have been, is, after all, only a means to an end. That end may be the capture of a portion of the ruins of the trench, it may be the destruction of an especially strong and dangerous 'keep,' a point of resistance or an angle for attack. It may even be a mine to destroy a mine which is known to be tunnelling into our own trenches, but in any case the explosion is usually a signal for attack from one side or the other, and therefore requires all the usual elaborate arrangements of reinforcements and supports and so on. Therefore the Sapper Subaltern, when he had finished his work and made his report, had nothing to do but sit down and wait until other people's preparations were made, and he received orders to complete his work by utterly and devastatingly destroying it. The Subaltern found this wait about the most trying part of the whole affair, more especially since he had for a good many days and nights had so much to occupy his every moment.

He received word at last of the day and hour appointed for the explosion, and had the honour of a visit of inspection from a very superior officer who pored long and painstakingly over the paper plans, put a great many questions, even went the length of walking down the communication trench and peering down the entrance shaft, and looking over the sandbagged wall through a periscope at the section of German trench marked down for destruction. Then he complimented the Subaltern on his work, declined once again the offer of a muddy mackintosh and an invitation to crawl down the mine, and went off. The Subaltern saw him off the premises, returned to the shaft and donned the mackintosh, and crawled off up his tunnel once more.

Somehow, now that the whole thing was finished and ready, he felt a pang of reluctance to destroy it and so fulfil its destiny. As he crawled along, he noted each little bit of shoring-up and supporting planks, each rise and fall in the floor, each twist and angle in the direction, and recalled the infinite labour of certain sections, his glows of satisfaction at the speed of progress at the easy bits, his impatience at the slow and difficult portions. It seemed as if he had been building that tunnel for half a lifetime, had hardly ever done anything else but build it or think about building it. And now, to-morrow it was all to be destroyed. He recalled with a thrill of boyish pleasure the word of praise from the Corporal--a far greater pleasure, by the way, than he had derived from the Great One's compliments--the praise of one artist to another, the recognition of good work done, by one who himself had helped in many good works and knew well of what he spoke. 'She's done, sir,' the Corporal had said. 'And if I may say so, sir, she's a credit to you. A mighty tricky job, sir, and I've seen plenty with long years in the Service that would ha' been stumped at times. I'm glad to have had a hand in it wi' you, sir. And all the men feel the same way about it.'

Ah well, the Subaltern thought as he halted at the joint of the T-piece, none of them felt the same about it as he himself did. He squatted there a moment, listening to the drip of water that was the only sound. Suddenly his heart leapt . . . was it the only sound? What was that other, if it could be called a sound? It was a sense rather, an indefinable blending of senses of hearing and feel and touch--a faint, barely perceptible 'thump, thump,' like the beat of a man's heart in his breast. He snapped off the light of his electric lamp and crouched breathless in the darkness, straining his ears to hear. He was soon satisfied. He had not lived these days past with the sound of digging in his ears by day and his dreams by night not to recognise the blows of a pick. There . . . they had stopped now; and in imagination he pictured the digger laying down the pick to shovel out the loosened earth. Then, after a pause, the measured thump, thump went on again. The Subaltern crawled along first one arm of the cross-section and then the other, halting every now and then to place his ear to the wet planking or the wetter earth. He located at last the point nearest to the sound, and without more waste of time scurried off down his tunnel to daylight.

He was back in the mine again in less than half an hour--a bare thirty minutes, but each minute close packed with concentrated essence of thought and action.

The nearest trench telephone had put him in touch with Battalion Headquarters, and through them with Brigade, Divisional, and General Headquarters. He had told his story and asked for his orders clearly, quickly, and concisely. The Germans were countermining. Their tunnel could not possibly miss ours, and, by the sound, would break through in thirty to sixty minutes. What were his orders? It took some little time for the orders to come, mainly because--although he knew nothing of it--his mine was part of a scheme for a general attack, and general attacks are affairs that cannot be postponed or expedited as easily as a cold lunch. But the Subaltern filled in the time of waiting, and when the orders did come he was ready for them or any other. They were clear and crisp--he was to fire the mine, but only at the latest possible minute. That was all he got, and indeed all he wanted; and, since they did not concern him, there is no need here to tell of the swirl of other orders that buzzed and ticked and talked by field telegraph and telephone for miles up and down and behind the British line.

Before these orders had begun to take shape or coherency as a whole, the Sub-altern was back listening to the thump, thump of the German picks, and busily completing his preparations. It was near noon, and perhaps the workers would stop for a meal, which would give another hour for troops to be pushed up or whatever else the Generals wanted time for. It might even be that a fall of their roof, an extra inflow of water to their working, any one of the scores of troubles that hamper and hinder underground mining might stop the crawling advance of the German sappers for a day or two and allow the Subaltern's mine to play its appointed part at the appointed time of the grand attack.

But meantime the Subaltern took no chances. First he connected up a short switch which in the last extreme of haste would allow him with one touch of his finger to blow up his mine and himself with it. He buried or concealed the wires connecting the linked charges with the switch outside so as to have a chance of escape himself. He opened a portable telephone he had carried with him and joined up to the wire he had also carried in, and so was in touch with his Corporal and the world of the aboveground. All these things he did himself because there was no need to risk more than one man in case of a quick explosion. Then, his preparations complete, he sat down to wait and to listen to the thudding picks of the Germans. They were very near now, and with his ear to the wall the Subaltern could hear the shovels now as well as the picks. He shut his lamp off after a last look at his switch, his revolver, and the glistening walls and mud-ooze floor of his tunnel, and sat still in the darkness. Once he whispered an answer into the telephone to his Corporal, and once he flicked his lamp on an instant to glance at the watch on his wrist. Then he crouched still and silent again. The thumping of his heart nearly drowned the thud of the picks, he was shivering with excitement, and his mouth grew dry and leathery. He felt a desire to smoke, and had his case out and a cigarette in his lips when it occurred to him that, when the Germans broke through, the smell of the smoke would tell them instantly that they were in an occupied working. He counted on a certain amount of delay and doubt on their part when their picks first pierced his wall, and he counted on that pause again to give him time to escape. So he put the cigarette away, and immediately was overwhelmed with a craving for it. He fought it for five minutes that felt like five hours, and felt his desire grow tenfold with each minute. It nearly drove him to doing what all the risk, all the discomfort of his cramped position, all the danger, had not done--to creep out and fire the mine without waiting for that last instant when the picks would break through. It could make little difference, he argued to himself, in the movements of those above. What could five minutes more, or ten, or even fifteen, matter now? It might even be that he was endangering the success of the explosion by waiting, and it was perhaps wiser to crawl out at once and fire the mine--and he could safely light a cigarette then as soon as he was round the corner of the T. So he argued the matter out, fingering his cigarette-case and longing for the taste of the tobacco, and yet knowing in his inmost heart that he would not move, despite his arguments, until the first pick came through. He heard the strokes draw nearer and nearer, and now he held his breath and strained his eyes as each one was delivered. The instant he had waited for came in exactly the fashion he had expected--a thud, a thread of yellow light piercing the black dark, a grunt of surprise from the pick-wielder at the lack of resistance to his stroke. All this was just what he had expected, had known would happen. The next stroke would show the digger that he was entering some hole. Then there would be cautious investigation, the sending back word to an officer, the slow and careful enlargement of the opening. And before that moment came the Subaltern would be down his tunnel, and outside, and pressing the switch . . .

But his programme worked out no further than that first instant and that first gleam of light. He saw the gleam widen suddenly as the pick was withdrawn, heard another quick blow, saw the round spot of light run out in little cracks and one wide rift, and suddenly the wall fell in, and he was staring straight into the German gallery, with a dark figure silhouetted clear down to the waist against the light of an electric bulb-lamp which hung from the gallery roof. For an instant the Subaltern's blood froze. The figure of the German was only separated from him by a bare three yards, and to his dark-blinded eyes it seemed that he himself was standing in plain view in a brilliant blaze of light. Actually he was in almost complete darkness. The single light in the German gallery hardly penetrated through the gloom of his own tunnel, and what little did showed nothing to the eyes of the German, used to the lamp-light and staring suddenly into the black rift before him. But the German called out to some one behind him, twisted round, moved, stooping, back to the lamp and reached up a hand to it. The Subaltern backed away hastily, his eyes fixed on the glow of light in the opening. The hole had broken through on a curve of his tunnel, so that for fifteen or twenty feet back he could still see down the German gallery, could watch the man unhook the lamp and carry it back to the opening, thrust the lamp before him and lean in over the crumbling heap of earth his pick had brought down. The Subaltern stopped and drew a gasping breath and held it. Discovery was a matter of seconds now. He had left his firing switch, but he still carried the portable telephone slung from his shoulder, the earth-pin dangling from it. He had only to thrust the pin into the mud and he was connected up with the Corporal at the outside switch, had only to shout one word, 'Fire!'--and it would all be over. Quickly but noiselessly he put his hand down to catch up the wire with the earth-pin. His hand touched the revolver-butt in his holster, checked at it, closed round it and slid it softly out. All this had taken an instant of time, and as he raised his weapon he saw the German still staring hard under the upheld lamp into the gloom. He was looking the other way, and the Subaltern levelled the heavy revolver and paused. The sights stood out clear and black against the figure standing in the glow of light--a perfect and unmissable target. The man was bareheaded, and wore a mud-stained blue shirt with sleeves cut off above the el- bow. The Subaltern moved the notched sights from under the armpit of the raised arm that held up the light, and steadied them on the round of the ear that stood out clear against the close-cropped black hair. He heard a guttural exclamation of wonder, saw the head come slowly round until the circle of the ear foreshortened and moved past his sights, and they were centred straight between the staring eyes. His finger contracted on the trigger, but a sudden qualm stayed him. It wasn't fair, it wasn't sporting, it was too like shooting a sitting hare. And the man hadn't seen him even yet. Man? This was no man; a lad rather, a youth, a mere boy, with child- ish wondering eyes, a smooth oval chin, the mouth of a pretty girl. The Subaltern had a school-boy brother hardly younger than this boy; and a quick vision rose of a German mother and sisters--no, he couldn't shoot; it would be murder; it--and then a quick start, an upward movement of the lamp, a sharp question, told him the boy had seen. The Subaltern spoke softly in fairly good German. 'Run away, my boy.

In an instant my mine will explode.'

'Who is it? Who is there?' gasped the boy.

The Subaltern chuckled, and grinned wickedly. Swiftly he dropped the revolver, fumbled a moment, and pulled a coil of capped fuse from his pocket.

'It is the English,' he said. 'It is an English mine that I now explode,' and, on the word, lit the fuse and flung it, fizzing and spitting a jet of sparks and smoke, towards the boy. The lad flinched back and half turned to run, but the Subaltern saw him look round over his shoulder and twist back, saw the eyes glaring at the fiery thing in the mud, the dreadful resolve grow swiftly on the set young face, the teeth clamped on the resolve. He was going to dash for the fuse, to try to wrench it out and, as he supposed, prevent the mine exploding. The Subaltern jerked up the revolver again. This would never do; the precious seconds were flying; at any moment another man might come. He would have saved this youngster if he could, but he could allow nothing to risk failure for his mine. 'Get back,' he said sharply. 'Get back quickly, or I shall shoot.'

But now what he had feared happened. A voice called, a scuffling footfall sounded in the German gallery, a dim figure pushed forward into the light beside the boy. The Subaltern saw that it was an officer, heard his angry oath in answer to the boy's quick words, his shout, 'The light, fool--break it'; saw the clenched fist's vicious buffet in the boyish face and the quick grab at the electric bulb. The Subaltern's revolver sights slid off the boy and hung an instant on the snarling face of the officer. . . .

In the confined space the roar of his heavy revolver rolled and thundered in reverberating echoes, the swirling powder-reek blinded him and stung in his nostrils; and as the smoke cleared he could see the boy scrambling back along his gallery and the officer sprawled face down across the earth-heap in the light of the fallen lamp.

The Subaltern smashed the lamp himself before he too turned and plunged, floundering and slipping and stumbling, for his exit in an agony of haste and apprehension. It was all right, he told himself a dozen times; the officer was done for--the back of that head and a past knowledge of a service revolver's work at close range told him that plain enough; it would take a good many minutes for the boy to tell his tale, and even then, if a party ventured back at once, it would take many more minutes in the dark--and he was glad he thought to smash the lamp--before they could find his charges or the wires. It was safe enough, but--the tunnel had never seemed so long or the going so slow. He banged against beams and supports, ploughed through sticky mud and churning water, rasped his knuckles, and bruised knees and elbows in his mad haste. It was safe enough, but--but--but--suppose there was no response to his pressure on the switch; suppose there had been some silly mistake in making the connections; suppose the battery wouldn't work. There were a score of things to go wrong. Thank goodness he had overhauled and examined everything himself; although that again would only make it more appallingly awful if things didn't work. No time now, no chance to go back and put things right. Perhaps he ought to have stayed back there and made the contact. A quick end if it worked right, and a last chance to refix it if it didn't; yes, he . . . but here was the light ahead. He shouted 'Fire!' at the top of his voice, still hurrying on and half cowering from the expected roar and shock of the explosion. Nothing happened. He shouted again and again as loud as his sobbing breath and labouring lungs would let him. Still--nothing; and it began to sear his brain as a dreadful certainty that he had failed, that his mine was a ghastly frost, that all the labour gone to its making and the good lives spent on it were wasted. He stumbled weakly out into the shaft, caught a glimpse of the Corporal's set face staring at the tunnel mouth, and tried once more to call out 'Fire!' But the Corporal was waiting for no word. He had already got that, had heard the Subaltern's first shouts roll down the tunnel, in fact was waiting with a finger on the exploding switch for the moment the Subaltern should appear. The finger moved steadily over as the Subaltern stumbled into sight--and the solid earth heaved convulsively, shuddered, and rocked and shook to the roaring blast of the explosion.

The shock and the rush of air from the tunnel-mouth caught the Subaltern, staggering to his knees, and flung him headlong. And as he picked himself up again the air darkened with whizzing clods and mud and dust and stones and dirt that rained down from the sky. Before the echoes of the explosion had died away, before the last fragments and debris had fallen, there came the sound of another roar, the bellowing thunder of the British guns throwing a storm of shell and shrapnel between the German supports and the ruined trench. That, and another sound, told the Subaltern that the full fruits of his work were to be fully reaped--the sound of the guns and of the full, deep-chested, roaring cheers of the British infantry as they swarmed from their trenches and rushed to occupy the crater of the explosion.

*   *   *   *   *

Later in the day, when the infantry had made good their possession of the place, had sandbagged and fortified it to stand against the expected counter-attacks, the Subaltern went to look over the ground and see at first and close hand the results of his explosion. Technically, he found it interesting; humanly, it was merely sickening. The ground was one weltering chaos and confusion of tossed earth-heaps and holes, of broken beams and jagged-ended planks, of flung sandbags and wrecked barricading. Of trench or barricade, as trench and barricade, there remained, simply, no sign. The wreckage was scattered thick with a dreadful debris of dead bodies, of bloody clothing, of helmets and broken rifles, burst packs and haversacks, bayonets, water-bottles, and shattered equipments. The Ambulance men were busy, but there were still many dead and dying and wounded to be removed, wounded with torn flesh and mangled limbs, dead and dying with scorched and smouldering clothes. The infantry, hastily digging and filling sandbags and throwing up parapets on the far edge of the reeking explosion pit, had found many bodies caught in the descending avalanche of earth or buried in the collapsed trenches and dug-outs; and here and there, amid the confusion, a foot or a hand protruding stark from some earth-heap marked the death-place of other victims. The whole scene was one of death and desolation, of ruin and destruction, and the Subaltern turned from it sick at stomach. It was the first result of a big explosion he had seen. This was the sort of thing that he had read so often summed up in a line of the Official Despatch or a two-line newspaper paragraph: 'A mine was successfully exploded under a section of the enemy's trench.' A mine--his mine. . . . 'God!' the Subaltern said softly under his breath, and looked wonderingly about him.

''E's a bloomin' little butcher, is that Lefftenant of ours,' the Corporal said that night. ''Course it was a good bit o' work, an' he'd reason to be proud of it; but--well I thought I'd a strongish stomach, an' I've seen some dirty blood-an'-bones messes in my time but that scorchin' shambles near turned me over. An' he comes back, after lookin' at it, as cheerful as the cornerman o' a Christie Minstrel troupe, an' as pleased as a dog wi' two tails. Fair pleased, 'e was.'

But he was a little wrong. What had brought the Subaltern back with such a cheerful air was not the sight of his work, not the grim picture of the smashed trenches. It was an encounter he had had with a little group of German prisoners, the recognising amongst them of a dirty, mud-stained blue shirt with sleeves cut off above the elbows, a close-cropped bare head, a boy's face with smooth oval chin and girlish eyes. The mine work he had directed, but others had shared it. It was the day's work--it was an incident of war--it was, after all, merely 'a mine successfully exploded . . .' But that one life saved was also his work, and, moreover, his own, his individual personal work. It was of that he thought most as he came back smiling to his Corporal.

ARTILLERY SUPPORT

'. . . supported by a close and accurate artillery fire . . .'--EXTRACT FROM OFFICIAL DESPATCH.

From his position in the 'Observation Post' the Artillery Forward Officer watched the fight raging along his front much as a spectator in the grandstand watches a football match. Through his glasses he could see every detail and movement of the fighters, see even their facial expressions, the grip of hands about their weapons. Queerly enough, it was something like looking at the dumb show of a cinema film. He could see a rifle pointed and the spit of flame from the muzzle without hearing any report, could see an officer gesticulating and his mouth opening and closing in obvious stentorian shoutings without hearing the faintest sound of his voice, could even see the quick flash and puffing smoke of a grenade without catching the crash of its explosion. It was not that he was too far off to hear all these sounds, but simply because individually they were drowned in the continuous ear-filling roar of the battle.

The struggle was keenly interesting and desperately exciting, even from a spectator's point of view; and the interest and excitement were the greater to the Forward Officer, because he was playing a part, and an important part, in the great game spread before him. Beyond the line of a section of the British front white smoke-puffs were constantly bursting, over his head a succession of shells streamed rushing and shrieking; and the place where each of those puffs burst depended on him, each shell that roared overhead came in answer to his call. He was 'observing' for a six-gun battery concealed behind a gentle slope over a mile away to his right rear, and, since the gunners at the battery could see nothing of the fight, nothing of their target, not even the burst of a single one of their shells, they depended solely on their Forward Officer to correct their aim and direct their fire.

All along the front--or rather both the fronts, for the German batteries worked on exactly the same system--the batteries were pouring down their shells, and each battery was dependent for the accuracy of its fire on its own Observing Officer crouching somewhere up in front and overlooking his battery's 'zone.'

The fighting line surged forward or swayed back, checked and halted, moved again, now rapidly, now slowly and staggeringly, curved forward here and dinted in there, striving fiercely to hold its ground in this place, driving forward in that, or breaking, reeling back into the arms of the supports, swirling forward with them again. But no matter whether the lines moved forward or back, fast or slow, raggedly and unevenly, or in one long close-locked line, ever and always the shells soared over and burst beyond the line, just far enough barely to clear it if the fight were at close quarters; reaching out and on a hundred, two hundred, yards when the fighters drew apart for a moment; always clear of their own infantry, and as exactly as possible on the fighting line of the enemy, for such is the essence of 'close and accurate artillery support.'

The Forward Observing Officer, perched precariously in an angle of the walls of a ruined cottage, stared through his glasses at the confusion of the fight for hour after hour until his eyes ached and his vision swam. The Forward Officer had been there since daybreak, and because no shells obviously aimed at his station had bombarded him--plenty of chance ones had come very close, but of course they didn't count--he was satisfied that he was reasonably secure, and told his Major back at the Battery so over his telephone. The succession of attack and counter-attack had ceased for the time being, and the Forward Officer let his glasses drop and shut his aching eyes for a moment. But, almost immediately, he had to open them and lift his head carefully, to peer out over the top of the broken wall; for the sudden crash of reopening rifle fire warned him that another move was coming. From far out on his left, beyond the range of his vision, the fire began. It beat down, wave upon wave, towards his front, crossed it, and went rolling on beyond his right. The initiative came from the British side, and, taking it as the prelude of an attack, developing perhaps out of sight on his left, the Forward Officer called up his Battery and quickened the rate of its fire upon the German line. In a few minutes he caught a quick stir in the British line, a glimpse of the row of khaki figures clambering from their trench and the flickering flash of their bayonets--and in an instant the flat ground beyond the trench was covered with running figures. They made a fair target that the German gunners, rifles, and maxims were quick to leap upon. The German trench streamed fire, the German shells--shrapnel and high-explosive--blew gaping rents in the running line. The line staggered and flinched, halted, recovered, and went on again, leaving the ground behind it dotted with sprawling figures. The space covered by the Forward Officer's zone was flat and bare of cover clear to the German trench two hundred yards away. It was too deadly a stretch for that gallant line to cover; and before it was half-way across, it faltered again, hung irresolute, and flung itself prone to ground. The level edge of the German trench suddenly became serrated with bobbing heads, flickered with moving figures, and the next moment was hidden by the swarm of men that leaped from it and came charging across the open. This line too withered and wilted under the fire that smote it, but it gathered itself and hurled on again. The Forward Officer called down the shortening ranges to the guns, and the answering shrapnel fell fiercely on the German line and tore it to fragments--but the fragments still advanced. The remnant of the British line rose and flung forward to meet it, and as the two clashed the supports from either side poured out to help. As the dense mass of Germans emerged, and knitted into close formation, the Forward Officer reeled off swift orders to the telephone. The shrieking tempest of his shells fell upon the mass, struck and slew wholesale, struck and slew again. The mass shivered and broke; but although part of it vanished back under the cover of the trench, although another part lay piled in a wreckage of dead and wounded, a third part straggled forward and charged into the fight. The British line was overborne, and pushed struggling back until new supports brought it fresh life and turned the tide again. The Germans surviving the charge were killed, wounded, or taken prisoners, and the Forward Officer, lifting his fire and pouring it on the German trench, checked for the moment any further rush of reinforcements. The British line ran forward to a field track running parallel to the trenches and nearly midway between them, flung itself down to escape the bullets that stormed across and began, as rapidly as the men's cramped position would allow, to dig themselves in. To their right and left the field track sank a foot or two below the surface of the field, and this scanty but precious shelter had allowed the rest of the line to stop half-way across and hold on to get its breath and allow a constant spray of supports to dash across the open and reinforce it. Now, the centre, where the track ran bare and flat across the field, plied frantic shovels to heap up some sort of cover that would allow them also to hang on in conformation of the whole line and gather breath and reinforcements for the next rush.

The Germans saw plainly enough what was the plan, and took instant steps to upset it. Their first and best chance was to thrust hard at the weak and ill-protected centre, overwhelm it and then roll up the lines to right and left of it.

A tornado of shell fire ushered in the new assault. The shells burst in running crashes up and down the advanced line, and up and down the British trench behind it; driving squalls of shrapnel swept the ground between the two, and, in addition, a storm of rifle and machine-gun bullets rained along the scanty parapet, whistled and droned and hissed across the open. And then, suddenly, the assault was launched from all along the German line.

At the same instant a shell struck the wall of the Forward Officer's station, burst with a terrific crash, swept three parts of the remaining wall away in a cloud of shrieking splinters and swirling dust of brick and plaster, and threw the Forward Officer headlong half a dozen yards. By some miracle he was untouched. His first thought was for the telephone--the connecting link with his guns. He scrambled over the debris to the dug-out or shelter-pit behind his corner and found telephonist and telephone intact. He dropped on hands and knees and crawled over the rubble and out beyond the end of the wall, for the cloud of smoke and plaster and brick-dust still hung heavily about the ruin. Here, in the open as he was, the air sang like tense harp-strings to the passage of innumerable bullets, the ground about his feet danced to their drumming, flicked and spat little spurts of mud all over him.

But the Forward Officer paid little heed to these things. For one moment his gaze was riveted horror-stricken on the scene of the fight; the next he was on his feet, heedless of the singing bullets, heedless of the roar and crash of another shell that hit the ground and flung a cart-load of earth and mud whizzing and thumping about him, heedless of everything except the need to get quickly to the telephone.

'Tell the Battery, Germans advancing--heavy attack on our front!' he panted to the telephonist, jumped across to his corner, and heaved himself up into place. The dust had cleared now, so that he could see. And what he could see made him catch his breath. An almost solid line of Germans were clear of their trenches and pushing rapidly across the open on the weak centre. And the Battery's shells were falling behind the German line and still on their trenches. Swiftly the Forward Officer began to reel off his corrections of angles and range, and as the telephonist passed them on gun after gun began to pitch its shells on the advancing line.

The British rifles were busy too, and their fire rose in one continuous roar. But the fire was weakest from the thin centre line, the spot where the attack was heaviest. The guns were in full play again, and the shells were blasting quick gaps out of the advancing line. But the line came on. The rifles beat upon it, and a machine-gun on the less heavily pressed left turned and mowed the Germans down in swathes. Still the line came on stubbornly. It was broken and ragged now, and advanced slowly, because the front ranks were constantly melting away under the British fire. The Forward Officer watched with straining eyes glued to his glasses. A shell 'whooped' past close over his head, and burst just beyond him. He neither turned his head nor moved his glasses. One, two, three, four burst short, and splinters and bullets sang past him; two more burst overhead, and the shrapnel clashed and rattled amongst the stone and brick of the ruins. Without moving, the Forward Officer began to call a fresh string of orders. The rush of his shells ceased for a moment while the gunners adjusted the new angles and ranges. 'Number One fired. Two fired. Three, Four, Five, Six fired, sir,' called the telephonist, and as he spoke there came the shrieks of the shells, and the white puffs of the bursts low down and between the prone British line and the advancing Germans.

'Number Three, one-oh minutes more left!' shouted the Forward Officer. 'Number Five, add twenty-five--repeat.'

Again came the running bursts and puffing white smoke, and satisfied this time with their line, position, and distance, the Forward Officer shouted for 'Gun-fire,' jumped down and across to the telephonist's shelter-pit.

'I'm putting a belt of fire just ahead of our line,' he shouted, curving his fingers about his lips and the mouthpiece in an attempt to shut out the uproar about them. 'If they can come through it we're done--infantry can't hold 'em. Give me every round you can, and as fast as you can, please.' He ran back to his place. A cataract of shells poured their shrapnel down along a line of which the nearest edge was a bare twenty yards from the British front. The Forward Officer fixed his eyes on the string of white smoke-puffs with their centre of winking flame that burst and burst and burst unceasingly. If one showed out of its proper place he shouted to the telephonist and named the delinquent gun, and asked for the lay and fuse-setting to be checked.

The advancing Germans reached at last the strip of ground where his shrapnel hailed and lashed, reached the strip and pushed into it--but not past it. Up to the shrapnel zone the advance could press; through, it could not. Under the shrapnel nothing could live. It swept the ground in driving gust on gust, swept and besomed it bare of life. Here and there, in ones and twos and little knots and groups, the Germans strove desperately to push on. They came as far as that deadly fire belt; and in ones and twos and little knots and groups they stayed there and died. Supports hurried up and hurled themselves in, and a spasm of fresh strength and fury lifted the line and heaved it forward. So far the fire of its fury brought it; and there the hosing shrapnel met it, swept down and washed it away, and beat it out to the last spark and the last man.

But from the German trenches another assault was forming, from the German batteries another squall of shell-fire smote the British line; and to his horror, the Forward Officer saw his own shells coming slower and slower, the smoke-bursts growing irregular and slower again. He leaped down and rushed to the telephone.

Back in the Battery the telephone wires ran into a dug-out that was the brain-centre of the guns, and from here the Forward Officer's directions emerged and were translated to the gunners through the Battery Commander and the Battery Sergeant-Major's megaphone.

All the morning the gunners followed those orders blindly, sluing the hot gun-muzzles a fraction this way or that, making minute adjustments on sights and range drums and shell fuses. They could see no glimpse of the fight, but, more or less accurately, they could follow its varying fortunes and trace its movements by the orders that came through to them. When they had to send their shells further back, the enemy obviously were being pressed back; when the fire had to be brought closer the enemy were closer. An urgent call for rapid fire with an increasing range meant our infantry attacking; with a lessening range, their being attacked.

Occasionally the Battery Commander passed to the Section Commanders items of news from the Forward Officer, and they in turn told the 'Numbers One' in charge of the guns, and the gun detachments.

Such a message was passed along when the Forward Officer telephoned news of the heavy pressure on the weakened centre. Every man in the Battery knew what was expected, and detachment vied with detachment in the speedy correcting of aim and range, and the rapid service of their guns. When the order came for a round of 'Battery fire'--which calls for the guns to fire in their turn from right to left--one gun was a few seconds late in reporting ready, and every other man at every other gun fretted and chafed impatiently as if each second had been an hour.

At another message from the Forward Officer the Battery Commander called for Section Commanders. The Sergeant-Major clapped megaphone to mouth and shouted, and two young subalterns and a sergeant jumped from their places, and raced for the dug-out. The Major spoke rapidly and tersely. 'We are putting down a belt of shrapnel in front of our own infantry--very close to them. You know what that means--the most careful and exact laying and fusing, and fire as hot and heavy as you can make it. The infantry can't hold 'em. They're depending on us; the line depends on us. Tell your men so. Be off, now.' The three saluted, whirled on their heels, and were off. They told their men, and the men strained every nerve to answer adequately to the call upon them. The rate of fire worked up faster and faster. Between the thunder-claps of the gun the Sergeant-Major's megaphone bellowed, 'Number Six, check your lay.' Number Six missed the message, but the nearest gun caught the word and passed it along. The Section Commander heard, saluted to show he had heard and understood, and ran himself to check the layer's aim.

Up to now the Battery had worked without coming under any serious fire. There were always plenty of rifle bullets coming over, and an occasional one of the shells that roared constantly past or over fell amongst the guns. A few men had been wounded, and one had been killed, and that was all.

Then, quite suddenly, a tempest of high-explosive shell rained down on the battery, in front of, behind, over, and amongst the guns. Instinctively the men hesitated in their work, but the next instant the voices of the Section Commanders brought them to themselves. There were shelter-pits and dug-outs close by, and, without urgent need of their fire, the guns might be left while the gunners took cover till the storm was over. But there could be no thought of that now, while the picture was in everyone's mind of the infantry out there being hard pressed and overborne by the weight of the assault. So the gunners stayed by their guns and loaded, laid, and fired as fast as they could serve their pieces. The gun shields give little or no protection from high-explosive shells, because these burst overhead and fling their fragments straight down, burst in rear, and hurl jagged splinters outwards in every direction. The men were as open and unprotected to them as bare flesh is to bullet or cold steel; but they knelt or sat in their places, and pushed their work into a speed that was only limited by the need for absolute accuracy.

A shell burst close in rear of Number One gun, and the whirlwind of splinters and bullets struck down half the detachment at a blow. The fallen men were lifted clear, the remaining gunners took up their appointed share of the lost men's duties, a shell was slung in, the breech slammed shut, the firing-lever jerked--and Number One gun was in action again and firing almost as fast as before. The sergeant in charge of another gun was killed instantaneously by a shrapnel bullet in the head. His place was taken by the next senior before the last convulsive tremors had passed through the dead man's muscles; and the gun kept on without missing a round.

The shell-fire grew more and more intense. The air was thick and choking with smoke and chemical fumes, and vibrant with the rush and shriek, of the shells, the hum of bullets, and the ugly whirr of splinters, the crash of impacting shells, and ear-splitting crack of the guns' discharge, the 'r-r-rupp' of shrapnel on the wet ground, the metallic clang of bullets and steel fragments on the gun-shields and mountings. But through all the inferno the gunners worked on, swiftly but methodically. After each shot the layers glared anxiously into the eye-piece of their sights and made minute movements of elevating and traversing wheels, the men at the range-drums examined them carefully and readjusted them exactly, the fuse-setters twisted the rings marking the fuse's time of burning until they were correct literally to a hair-line; every man working as if the gun were shooting for a prize-competition cup. Their care, as well as their speed, was needed; for, more than any cup, good men's lives were at stake and hanging on their close and accurate shooting. For if the sights were a shade to right or left of their 'aiming point,' if the range were shortened by a fractional turn of the drum, if a fuse was wrongly set to one of the scores of tiny marks on its ring, that shell might fall on the British line, take toll of the lives of friend instead of foe, go to break down the hard-pressed British resistance instead of upholding it.

Man after man was hit by shell splinter or bullet, but no man left his place unless he was too badly injured to carry on. The seriously wounded dragged themselves clear as best they could and crawled to any cover from the bursting shells; the dead lay where they fell. The detachments were reduced to skeleton crews. One Section Commander laid and fired a gun; another, with a smashed thigh, sat and set fuses until he fainted from loss of blood and from pain. The Battery Commander took the telephone himself and sent the telephonist to help the guns; and when a bursting shell tore out one side of the sandbags of the dug-out the Battery Commander rescued himself and the instrument from the wreckage, mended the broken wire, and sat in the open, alternately listening at the receiver and yelling exhortation and advice to the gunners through the Sergeant-Major's megaphone. The Sergeant-Major had gone on the run to round up every available man, and brought back at the double the Battery cooks, officers' grooms, mess orderlies and servants. The slackening fire of the Battery spurted again and ran up to something like its own rate. And the Major cheered the men on to a last effort, shouting the Forward Officer's message that the attack was failing, was breaking, was being wiped out mainly by the Battery's fire. And then, as suddenly as it had begun, the tornado of shell-fire about them ceased, shifted its storm-centre, and fell roaring and crashing and hammering on an empty hedge and ditch a full three hundred yards away.

And at the same moment the Major shouted exultingly. 'They're done!' he bellowed down the megaphone; 'they're beat! The attack--and he fell back on the Forward Officer's own words--'the attack is blotted out.'

Whereat the panting gunners cheered faintly and short-windedly, and took contentedly the following string of orders to lengthen the range and slacken the rate of fire. And the Battery made shift to move its dead from amongst the gun and wagon wheels, to bandage and tie up its wounded with 'first field dressings,' to shuffle and sort the detachments and redistribute the remaining men in fair proportion amongst the remaining guns, to telephone the Brigade Headquarters to ask for stretcher-bearers and ambulance, and more shells--doing it all, as it were, with one hand while the other kept the guns going, and the shells pounding down their appointed paths.

For the doing of two or more things at once, and doing them rapidly, exactly, and efficiently, the while in addition highly unpleasant things are being done to them, is all a part of the Gunners' game of 'close and accurate artillery support.'

'NOTHING TO REPORT'

'On the Western Front there is nothing to report. All remains quiet.'--OF-FICIAL DESPATCH.

The 7th (Territorial) King's Own Asterisks had 'taken over' their allotted portion of the trenches and were settling themselves in for the night. When the two facts are taken in conjunction that it was an extremely unpleasant night, cold, wet and bleak, and the 7th were thoroughly happy and would not have exchanged places with any other battalion in Flanders, it will be very plain to those who know their Front that the 7th K.O.A. were exceedingly new to the game. They were: and actually this was their first spell of duty in the forward firing trenches.

They had been out for some weeks, weary weeks, filled with the digging of communication trenches well behind the firing trenches, with drills and with various 'fatigues' of what they considered a navvying rather than a military nature. But every task piled upon their reluctant shoulders had been performed promptly and efficiently, and now at last they were enjoying the reward of their zeal--a turn in the forward trenches.

The men were unfeignedly pleased with themselves, with the British Army, and with the whole world. The non-coms, were anxious and desperately keen to see everything in apple-pie order. The Company officers were inclined to be fidgety, and the O.C. was worried and concerned to the verge of nerves. He pored over the trench maps that had been handed to him, he imagined assaults delivered on this point and that, hurried, at the point of the pencil, his supports along various blue and red lines to the threatened angles of the wriggly line that represented the forward trench, drew lines from his machine-gun emplacements to the red-inked crosses of the German wire entanglements, frowned and cogitated over the pencil crosses placed by the O.C. of the relieved battalion where the lurking-places of German maxims were suspected. Afterwards he made a long and exhaustive tour of the muddy trenches, concealing his anxiety from the junior officers, and speaking lightly and cheerfully to them--following therein truly and instinctively the first principle of all good commanders to show the greater confidence as they feel it the less. He returned to the Battalion Headquarters, situated in a very grimy cellar of a shell-wrecked house behind the support trenches, and partook of a belated dinner of tinned food flavoured with grit and plaster dust.

The signallers were established with their telephones at the foot of the stone stair outside the cellar door, and into this cramped 'exchange' ran the telephone wires from the companies in the trenches and from the Brigade Headquarters a mile or two back. Every word that the signallers spoke was plainly heard in the cellar, and every time the Colonel heard 'Hello! Yes, this is H.Q.,' he sat motionless waiting to hear what message was coming through. When his meal was finished he resisted an impulse to 'phone' all the forward trenches, asking how things were, unlaced his boots, paused, and laced them up again, lay down on a very gritty mattress in a corner of the cellar, and tried to sleep. For the first hour every rattle of rifle fire, every thud of a gun, every call on the telephone brought him up on his pillow, his ears straining to catch any further sound. After about the tenth alarm he reasoned the matter out with himself something after this fashion:--

'The battalion is occupying a position that has not been attacked for weeks, and it is disposed as other Regular battalions have been, and no more and no less effectually than they. There isn't an officer or man in the forward trenches who cannot be fully trusted to keep a look-out and to resist an attack to the last breath. There is no need to worry or keep awake, and to do so is practically admitting a distrust of the 7th K.O.A. I trust them fully, and therefore I ought to go to sleep.'

Whereupon the Colonel sat up, took off his wet boots, lay down again, resolutely closed his eyes--and remained wide awake for the rest of the night.

But if there be any who feel inclined to smile at the nervousness of an elderly, stoutish, and constitutionally easy-going Colonel of Territorials, I would remind them of a few facts. The Colonel had implicit faith in the stout-heartedness, the spirit, the fighting quality of his battalion. He had had the handling and the training of them ever since mobilisation, and he knew every single man of them as well as they knew themselves. They had done everything asked of them and borne light-heartedly rough quarters, bad weather, hard duties. But--and one must admit it a big and serious 'but'--to-night might be their real and their first testing in the flame and fire of War.

Even as no man knows how he will feel and behave under fire, until he has been under fire, so no regiment or battalion knows. The men were razor-keen for action, but that very keenness might lead them into a rashness, a foolhardiness, which would precipitate action. The Colonel believed they would stand and fight to the last gasp and die to the last man rather than yield a yard of their trench. He believed that of them even as he believed it of himself--but he did not know it of them any more than he knew it of himself. Men, apparently every bit as good as him, had before now developed some 'white streak,' some folly, some stupidity, in the stress and strain of action. Other regiments, apparently as sound as his, had in the records of history failed or broken in a crisis. He and his were new and untried, and military commanders for innumerable ages had doubted and mistrusted new and untried troops.

Well . . . he had done his best, and at least the next twenty-four hours should show him how good or how bad that best had been. But meantime let no one blame him for his anxiety or nervousness.

And meantime the 7th Asterisks, serenely unaware of their Commanding Officer's worry and doubt--and to be fair to them and to him it must be stated that they would have flouted scornfully any suggestion that he had held them--joyfully set about the impossible task of making themselves comfortable, and the congenial one of making the enemy extremely uncomfortable. The sentries were duly posted, and spent an entirely unnecessary proportion of their time peering over the parapet.

There were more Verey pistol lights burnt during the night than would have sufficed a trench-hardened battalion for a month, and the Germans opposite, having in hand a little job of adding to their barbed-wire defences, were puzzled and rather annoyed by the unwonted display of fireworks. They foolishly vented their annoyance by letting off a few rounds of rapid fire at the opposition, and the 7th Asterisks eagerly accepted the challenge, manned their parapets and proceeded to pour a perfect hurricane of fire back to the challengers. The Germans, with the exception of about a dozen picked sharp-shooting snipers, ceased to fire and took careful cover.

The snipers, daring the Asterisks' three minutes of activity, succeeded in scoring seven hits, and the Asterisks found themselves in possession of a casualty list of one killed and six wounded before the Company and platoon commanders had managed to stop the shooting and get the men down under cover.

When the shooting had ceased and the casualties had been cleared out on their way to the dressing station, the Asterisks recharged their rifle-magazines and spent a good hour discussing the incident, those men who had been beside the casualties finding themselves and their narratives of how it happened in great demand.

And one of the casualties, having insisted, when his slight wound was dressed, on returning to the trench, had to deliver a series of lecturettes on what it felt like, what the Medical said, how the other fellows were, how the dressing station was worked, and similar subjects, with pantomimic illustrations of how he was holding his rifle when the bullet came through the loophole, and how he was still fully capable of continuing to hold it.

A heavy shower dispersed the audiences, those of the men who were free to do so returning to muddy and leaky dug-outs, and the remainder taking up their positions at the parapet. There was as much chance of these latter standing on their heads as there was of their going to sleep, but the officers made so many visiting rounds to be certain of their sentries' wakefulness, and spent so long on each round and on the fascinating peeps over into 'the neutral ground,' that the end of one round was hardly completed before it was time to begin the next.

Occasionally the Germans sent up a flare, and every man and officer of the K.O.A. who was awake stared out through the loopholes in expectation of they knew not what. They also fired off a good many 'pistol lights,' and it was nearly 4 A.M. before the Germans ventured to send out their working-party over the parapet. Once over, they followed the usual routine, throwing themselves flat in the mud and rank grass when a light flared up and remaining motionless until it died out, springing to silent and nervous activity the instant darkness fell, working mostly by sense of touch, and keeping one eye always on the British parapet for the first hint of a soaring light.

The 'neutral ground' between the trenches was fairly thickly scattered over with dead, the majority of them German, and it was easy enough for an extra score or so of men, lying prone and motionless as the dead themselves, to be overlooked in the shifting light. The work was proceeding satisfactorily and was almost completed when a mischance led to the exposure of the party.

One of the workers was in the very act of crawling over the parapet when a British light flared. Half-way over he hesitated one moment whether to leap back or forward, then hurriedly leapt down in front of the parapet and flung himself flat on his face. He was just too late. The lights revealed him exactly as he leapt, and a wildly excited King's Own Asterisk pulled back the cut-off of his magazine and opened rapid fire, yelling frenziedly at the same time that they were coming--were coming--were attacking--were charging--look out!

Every K.O.A. on his feet lost no time in joining in the 'mad minute' and every K.O.A. who had been asleep or lying down was up in a twinkling and blazing over the parapet before his eyes were properly opened. The machine-gun detachment were more circumspect if no less eager. The screen before the wide loophole was jerked away and the fat barrel of the maxim peered out and swung smoothly from side to side, looking for a fair mark.

It had not long to wait. The German working-party 'stuck it out' for a couple of minutes, but with light after light flaming into the sky and exposing them pitilessly, with the British trench crackling and spitting fire from end to end, with the bullets hissing and whistling over them, and hailing thick amongst them, their nerves gave and broke; in a frantic desire for life and safety they flung away the last chance of life and safety their prone and motionless position gave them.

They scrambled to their feet, a score of long-cloaked, crouching figures, glaringly plain and distinct in the vivid light, and turned to run for their trench. The sheeting bullets caught half a dozen and dropped them before they had well stood up, stumbled another two or three over before they could stir a couple of paces, went on cutting down the remainder swiftly and mercilessly. The remainder ran, stumbling and tripping and staggering, their legs hampered by their long coats, their feet clogged and slipping in the wet, greasy mud. The eye glaring behind the swinging sights of the maxim caught that clear target of running figures, the muzzle began to jet forth a stream of fire and hissing bullets, the cartridge belt to click, racing through the breach.

The bullets cut a path of flying mud-splashes across the bare ground to the runners, played a moment about their feet, then lifted and swept across and across- -once, twice, thrice. On the first sweep the thudding bullets found their targets, on the second they still caught some of them, on the third they sang clear across and into the parapet, for no figures were left to check their flight. The working party was wiped out.

It took the excited riflemen another minute or two to realise that there was nothing left to shoot at except an empty parapet and some heaps of huddled forms; but the pause to refill the empty magazines steadied them, and then the fire died away.

The whole thing was over so quickly that the rifle fire had practically ceased before the Artillery behind had time to get to work, and by the time they had flung a few shells to burst in thunder and lightning roar and flash over the German parapet, the storm of rifle fire had slackened and passed. Hearing it die away, the gunners also stopped, reloaded, and laid their pieces, waited the reports of their Forward Officers, and on receiving them turned into their dug-outs and their blankets again.

But the batteries covering the front held by the Asterisks remained by their guns and continued to throw occasional rounds into the German trenches. Their Forward Officers had passed on the word received from the Asterisks of a sharp attack quickly beaten back--that being the natural conclusion drawn from that leaping figure on the parapet and the presence of Germans in the open--and the guns kept up a slow rate of fire more with the idea of showing the enemy that the defence was awake and waiting for them than of breaking up another possible attack. The battalions of Regulars to either side of the Asterisks had more correctly diagnosed the situation as 'false alarm' or 'ten rounds rapid on working parties,' and their supporting Artillery did no more than carry on their usual night firing.

The result of it all was that the Asterisks throughout the night enjoyed the spectacle of some very pretty artillery fire in the dark on and over the trenches facing them, and also the much less pleasing one of German shells bursting in the British trenches, and especially in those of the K.O.A. They had the heaviest share on the simple and usual principle of retaliation, whereby if our Section A of trenches is shelled we shell the German section facing it, and *vice versa*.

The fire was by no means heavy as artillery fire goes these days, and at first the

Asterisks were not greatly disturbed by it. But even a rate of three or four shells every ten or fifteen minutes is galling, and necessitates the keeping of close cover or the loss of a fair number of men. It took half a dozen casualties to impress firmly on the Asterisks the need of keeping cover. Shell casualties have an extremely ugly look, and some of the Asterisks felt decidedly squeamish at sight of theirs--especially of one where the casualty had to be collected piece by piece, and removed in a sack.

For an hour before dawn the battalion 'stood to,' lining the trench with loaded rifles ready after the usual and accepted fashion, shivering despite their warm clothing and mufflers, and woollen caps and thick great-coats in the raw-edged cold of the breaking day. For an hour they stood there listening to the whine of overhead bullets and the sharp 'slap' of well-aimed ones in the parapet, the swish and crash of shells, the distant patter of rifle fire and the boom of the guns.

That hour is perhaps always the worst of the twenty-four. The rousing from sleep, the turning out from warm or even from wet blankets, the standing still in a water-logged trench, with everything--fingers and clothes and rifle and trench-sides--cold and wet and clammy to the touch, and smeared with sticky mud and clay, all combine to make the morning 'stand to arms' an experience that no amount of repetition ever accustoms one to or makes more bearable.

Even the Asterisks, fresh and keen and enthusiastic as they were, with all the interest that novelty gave to the proceedings, found the hour long-drawn and trying; and it was with intense relief that they saw the frequently consulted watches mark the finish of the time, and received the word to break off from their vigil.

They set about lighting fires and boiling water for tea, and frying a meagre bacon ration in their mess-tin lids, preparing and eating their breakfast. The meal over, they began on their ordinary routine work of daily trench life.

Picked men were told off as snipers to worry and harass the enemy. They were posted at loopholes and in various positions that commanded a good outlook, and they fired carefully and deliberately at loopholes in the enemy parapet, at doors and windows of more or less wrecked buildings in rear of the German lines, at any and every head or hand that showed above the German parapet. In the intervals of firing they searched through their glasses every foot of parapet, every yard of ground, every tree or bush, hayrick or broken building that looked a likely spot to make cover for a sniper on the other side. If their eye caught the flash of a rifle, the instantly vanishing spurt of haze or hot air--too thin and filmy to be called smoke--that spot was marked down, long and careful search made for the hidden sniper, and a sort of Bisley 'disappearing target' shoot commenced, until the opponent was either hit or driven to abandon his position.

The enemy's snipers were, of course, playing exactly the same game, and either because they were more adept at it, or because the Asterisks' snipers were more reluctant to give up a position after it was 'spotted' and hung on gamely, determined to fight it out, a slow but steady tally was added to the Asterisks' casualty list.

Along the firing and communication trenches parties set to work of various sorts, bailing out water from the trench bottom, putting in brushwood or brick foundations, building up and strengthening dug-outs and parapets, filling sandbags in readiness for night work and repairs on any portion damaged by shell fire.

By now they were learning to keep well below the parapet, not to linger in portions of the communication trench that were enfiladed by shrapnel, to stoop low and pass quickly at exposed spots where the snipers waited a chance to catch an unwary head. They had learned to press close and flat against the face of the trench or to get well down at the first hint of the warning rush of an approaching shell; they were picking up neatly and quickly all the worst danger spots and angles and corners to be avoided except in time of urgent need.

One thing more was needed to complete their education in the routine of trench warfare, and the one thing came about noon just as the Asterisks were beginning to feel pleasant anticipations of the dinner hour. A faint and rather insignificant 'bang' sounded out in front. The Asterisks never even noticed it, but next moment when something fell with a thudding 'splosh' on the wet ground behind the trench the men nearest the spot lifted their heads and stared curiously. Another instant and with a thunderous roar and a leaping cloud of thick smoke the bomb burst. The men ducked hastily, but one or two were not quick enough or lucky enough to escape, although at that short distance they were certainly lucky in escaping with nothing worse than flesh wounds from the fragments of old iron, nails and metal splinters that whirled outwards in a circle from the bursting bomb. Everyone heard the second shot and many saw the bomb come over in a high curve.

As it dropped it appeared to be coming straight down into the trench and every man had an uncomfortable feeling that the thing was going to fall directly on him. Actually it fell short and well out in front of the trench and only a few splinters and a shower of earth whizzed over harmlessly high.

The third was another 'over' and the fourth another 'short' and the Asterisks, unaware of the significance of the closing-in 'bracket' began to feel relief and a trifle of contempt for this clumsy slow-moving and visible missile. Their relief and contempt vanished for ever when the fifth bomb fell exactly in the trench, burst with a nerve-shattering roar, and filled the air with whistling fragments and dense choking, blinding smoke and stench.

Having got their range and angle accurately, the Germans proceeded to hurl bomb after bomb with the most horrible exactness and persistency. For two hundred yards up and down the trench there was no escape from the blast of the bursts. It was no good crouching low, or flattening up against the parapet; for the bombs dropped straight down and struck out backwards and sideways and in every direction.

Even the roofed-in dug-outs gave no security. A bomb that fell just outside the entrance of one dug-out, riddled one man lying inside, and blew another who was crouching in the entrance outwards bodily across the trench, stunning him with the shock and injuring him in a score of places. Plenty of the bombs fell short of the trench, but too many fell fairly in it. When one did so there was only one thing to do--to throw oneself violently down in the mud of the trench bottom, and wait, heart in mouth, for the crash of the explosion.

The Artillery, on being appealed to, pounded the front German trench for an hour, but made no impression on the trench-mortar. The O.C. of the Asterisks telephoned the Brigade asking what he was to do to stop the torment and destruction, and in reply was told he ought to bomb back at the bomb-throwers. But the Asterisks had already tried that without any success. The distance was too great for hand bombs to reach, and the men appeared to make poor shooting with the rifle grenades.

'Why not try the trench-mortar?' asked the Brigade; to which the harassed Colonel replied conclusively because he didn't possess one, hadn't a bomb for one, and hadn't a man or officer who knew how to use one.

The Brigade apparently learnt this with surprise, and replied vaguely that steps would be taken, and that an officer and detachment of his battalion must receive a course of instruction.

The Colonel replied with spirit that he was glad to hear all this, but in the meantime what was he to do to prevent his battalion being blown piecemeal out of their trenches?

It all ended eventually in the arrival of a trench-mortar and a pile of bombs from somewhere and a very youthful and very much annoyed Artillery subaltern from somewhere else. The Colonel was most enormously relieved by these arrivals, but his high hopes were a good deal dashed by the artilleryman.

That youth explained that he was in effect totally ignorant of trench-mortars and their ways, that he had been shown the thing a week ago, had it explained to him--so far as such a rotten toy could be explained--and had fired two shots from it. However, he said briskly, if off-handedly, he was ready to have a go with it and see what he could do.

The trench-mortar was carried down to the forward trench, and on the way down behind it the youngster discoursed to the O.C. of the Asterisks on the 'awful rot' of a gunner officer being chased off on to a job like this--any knowledge of gunnery being entirely superfluous and, indeed, wasted on such a kid's toy. And the O.C., looking at the trench-mortar being prepared, made a mental remark about 'the mouths of babes' and the wise words thereof.

The weapon is easily described. It was a mere cylinder of cast iron, closed at one end, open at the other, and with a roomy 'touch-hole' at the closed end. The carriage consisted of two uprights on a base, with mortar between them and pointing up at an angle of about forty-five degrees.

The charge was little packets of gunpowder tied up in paper in measured doses. The bomb was a tin-can--an empty jam-tin, mostly--filled with a bursting charge and fragments of metal, and with an inch or so of the fuse protruding.

The piece was loaded by throwing a few packets of powder into the muzzle, poking them with a piece of stick to burst the paper, and carefully sliding the bomb down on top of the charge. A length of fuse was poked into the touch-hole and the end lit, sufficient length being given to allow the lighter to get round the nearest corner before the mortar fired.

The whole thing was too rubbishy and cheaply and roughly made to have been fit for use as a 'kid's toy,' as the subaltern called it. To imagine it being used as a weapon of precision in a war distinguished above all others as one of scientifically perfect weapons and implements was ridiculous beyond words.

The Colonel watched the business of loading and laying with amazement and consternation.

'Is it possible to--er--hit anything with that?' he asked.

'Well, more or less,' said the youthful subaltern doubtfully. 'There's a certain amount of luck about it, I believe.'

'But why on earth,' said the Colonel, beginning to wax indignant, 'do they send such a museum relic here to fight a reasonably accurate and decidedly destructive mortar?'

The subaltern chuckled.

'That's not any museum antique,' he said. 'That's a Mortar, Trench, Mark Something or other--the latest, the most modern weapon of the kind in the British Army. It was made, I believe, in the Royal Arsenal, and it is still being made and issued for use in the field--the Engineers collecting the empty jam-pots and converting them to bombs. They've only had four or five months, y'see, to evolve a---- look out, sir! Here's one of theirs!'

The resulting explosion flung a good deal of mud over the parapet on to the Colonel and the subaltern, and raised the youth to wrath.

'Beasts!' he said angrily, and poked a length of fuse in the touch-hole. 'Get away round the traverse!' he ordered the mob near him. 'And you'd better go, too, sir--as I will when I've touched her off. Y'see, she's just as liable to explode as not, and, if she does, she'd make more mess in this trench than I can ever hope she will in a German one.'

The Colonel retired round the nearest traverse, and next moment the lieutenant plunged round after him just as the mortar went off with a resounding bang. Every man in the trench watched the bomb rise, twirling and twisting, and fall again, turning end over end towards the German trench.

At about the moment he judged it should burst, the lieutenant poked his head up over the parapet, but bobbed down hurriedly as a couple of bullets sang past his ear.

'Pretty nippy lot across there!' he said. 'I must find a loophole to observe from.

And p'r'aps you'd tell some of your people to keep up a brisk fire on that parapet to stop 'em aiming too easy at me. Now we'll try another.'

At the next bang from the opposite trench he risked another quick peep over and this time ducked down with an exclamation of delight.

'I've spotted him.' he said. 'Just caught the haze of his smoke. Down the trench about fifty yards. So we'll try trail-left a piece--or would if this old drain-pipe had a trail.'

He relaid his mortar carefully, and fired again. Having no sights or arrangement whatever for laying beyond a general look over the line of its barrel and a pinch more or less of powder in the charge, it can only be called a piece of astounding good luck that the jam-pot bomb fell almost fairly on the top of the German mortar. There was a most satisfying uproar and eddying volume of smoke and eruption of earth, and the lieutenant stared through a loophole dumb-founded with delight.

'I'll swear,' he said, 'that our old Plum-and-Apple pot never made a burst that big. I do believe it must have flopped down on the other fellow and blown up one or two of his bombs same time. I say, isn't that the most gorgeous good luck? Well, good enough to go on with. We'll have a chance for some peaceful practice now?'

Apparently, since the other mortar ceased to fire, it must have been put out of action, and the lieutenant spent a useful hour pot-shotting at the other trench.

The shooting was, to say the least, erratic. With apparently the same charge and the same tilt on the mortar, one bomb would drop yards short and another yards over. If one in three went within three yards of the trench, if one in six fell in the trench, it was, according to the lieutenant, a high average, and as much as any man had a right to expect. But at the end of the hour, the Asterisks, who had been hugely enjoying the performance, and particularly the cessation of German bombs, were horrified to hear a double report from the German trench, and to see two dark blobs fall twinkling from the sky.

The following hour was a nightmare. Their trench-mortar was completely out-shot. Those fiendish bombs rained down one after the other along the trench, burst in devastating circles of flame and smoke and whirling metal here, there, and everywhere.

The lieutenant replied gallantly. A dozen times he had to shift position, because he was obviously located, and was being deliberately bombarded.

But at last the gunner officer had to retire from the contest. His mortar showed distinct signs of going to pieces--the muzzle-end having begun to split and crack, and the breech-end swelling in a dangerous-looking bulge.

'Look at her,' said the lieutenant disgustedly. 'Look at her opening out an' unfolding herself like a split-lipped ox-eyed daisy. Anyhow, this is my last bomb, so the performance must close down till we get some more jam-pots loaded up.'

The enemy mortars were evidently of better make, for they continued to bombard the suffering Asterisks for another full hour. They did a fair amount of damage to the trench and parapet, and the Germans seized the opportunity of the Asterisks' attempted repairs to put in some maxim practice and a few rounds of shrapnel.

Altogether, the 7th King's Own Asterisks had a lively twenty-four hours of it, and their casualties were heavy, far beyond the average of an ordinary day's trench work. Forty-seven they totalled in all--nine killed and thirty-six wounded.

They were relieved that night, this short spell being designed as a sort of introduction or breaking in or blooding to the game.

Taking it all round, the Asterisks were fully pleased with themselves. Their Colonel had complimented them on their behaviour, and they spent the next few days back in the reserve, speculating on what the papers would say about them. The optimists were positive they would have a full column at least.

'We beat on an attack,' they said. 'There's sure to be a bit in about that. And look at the way we were shelled, and our Artillery shelled back. There was a pretty fair imitation of a first-class battle for a bit, and most likely there would have been one if we hadn't scuppered that attack. And don't forget the bombing we stuck out--and the casualties. Doesn't every one tell us they were extra heavy? And I believe we are about the first Terrier lot to be in a heavy "do" in the forward trenches. You see--it'll be a column at least, and may be two.'

The pessimists declared that two or three paragraphs were all they could expect, on account of the silly fashion of not publishing details of engagements. 'And whatever mention we do get,' they said, 'won't say a word about the K.O.A. It'll just be a "battalion," or maybe "a Territorial battalion," and no more.'

'Anyway,' said the optimists, 'we'll be able to write home to our people and our pals, and tell them it was us, though the despatches don't mention us by name.'

But optimists and pessimists alike grabbed the papers that came to hand each day, and searched eagerly for the Eye-witness' reports, or the official despatch or communique. At last there reached them the paper with the communique dated the day after their day in the trenches. They stared at it, and then hurried over the other pages, turned back, and examined them carefully one by one. There were columns and columns about a strike and other purely domestic matters at home, but not a word about the 7th Kings Own Asterisks (Territorial), not a word about their nine dead and thirty-six wounded--not a word; and, more than that, barely a word about the Army, or the Front, or the War.

'There might be no bloomin' war at all to look at this paper,' said one in disgust. 'There's plenty about speeding-up the factories (an' it's about time they speeded up some one to make something better'n that drain-pipe or jam-pot bomb we saw), plenty about those loafin' swine at home, but not a bloomin' word about us 'ere. It makes me fair sick.'

'P'raps there wasn't time to get it in,' suggested one of the most persistent optimists. 'P'raps they'll have it in to-morrow.'

'P'raps,' said the disgusted one contemptuously, 'an' p'raps not. Look at the date of that despatch. Isn't that for the day we was in the thick of it? An' look what it says. Don't that make you sick?'

And in truth it did make them 'sick.' For their night and day of fighting--their defeat of an attack, their suffering under shell, bullet, and bomb, their nine killed and their thirty-six wounded--were all ignored and passed by.

The despatch for that day said simply: 'On the Western Front there is nothing to report. All remains quiet.'

THE PROMISE OF SPRING

'Only when the fields and roads are sufficiently dry will the favourable moment have come for an advance.'--EXTRACT FROM OFFICIAL DESPATCH.

It is Sunday, and the regiment marching out towards the firing line and its turn of duty in the trenches meets on the road every now and then a peasant woman on her way to church. Some of the women are young and pretty, some old and wrinkled and worn; they walk alone or in couples or threes, but all alike are dressed in black, and all alike tramp slowly, dully, without spring to their step. Over them the sun shines in a blue sky, round them the birds sing and the trees and fields spread green and fresh; the flush of healthy spring is on the countryside, the promise of warm, full-blooded summer pulses in the air. But there is no hint of spring or summer in the sad-eyed faces or the listless, slow movements of the women. It is a full dozen miles to the firing line, and to eye or ear, unless one knows where and how to look and listen, there is no sign of anything but peace and pleasant life in the surroundings. But these black-clad women do know--know that the cool green clump of trees over on the hill-side hides a roofless ruin with fire-blackened walls; that the church spire that for all their lives they had seen out there over the sky-line is no longer visible because it lies shell-smitten to a tumbled heap of brick and stone and mortar; that the glint of white wood and spot of scarlet yonder in the field is the rough wooden cross with a *kepi* on top marking the grave of a soldier of France; that down in the hollow just out of sight are over a score of those cap-crowned crosses; that a broad belt of those graves runs unbroken across this sunlit face of France. They know, too, that those dull booms that travel faintly to the ear are telling plain of more graves and of more women that will wear black.

It is little wonder that there are few smiles to be seen on the faces of these women by the wayside. They have seen and heard the red wrath of war, not in the pictures of the illustrated papers, not in the cinema shows, not even by the word-of-mouth tales of chance men who have been in it; but at first-hand, with their own eyes and ears, in the leaping flames of burning homes, in the puffing white clouds of the shrapnel, the black spouting smoke of the high-explosive, in the deafening thunder of the guns, the yelling shells, the crash of falling walls, the groans of wounded men, the screams of frightened children. Some of them may have seen the shattered hulks of men borne past on the sagging stretchers; all of them have seen the laden ambulance wagons and motors crawling slowly back to the hospitals.

And of these women you do not say, as you would of our women at home, that they may perhaps have friend or relation, a son, a brother, a husband, a lover, at the front. You say with certainty they have one or other of these, and may have all, that every man they know, of an age between, say, eighteen and forty, is serving his country in the field or in the workshops--and mostly in the field--if so be they are still alive to serve.

The men in the marching khaki regiment know all these things, and there are respect and sympathy in the glances and the greetings that pass from them to the women. 'They're good plucked 'uns,' they tell each other, and wonder how our women at home would shape at this game, and whether they would go on living in a house that was next door to one blown to pieces by a shell yesterday, and keep on working in fields where hardly a day passed without a shell screaming overhead, whether they'd still go about their work as best they could for six days a week and then to church on Sunday.

Two women, one young and lissom, the other bent and frail and clinging with her old arm to the erect figure beside her, stand aside close to the ditch and watch the regiment tramp by. 'Cheer up, mother,' one man calls. 'We're goin' to shift the Boshies out for you,' and 'Bong jewer,' says another, waving his hand. Another pulls a sprig of lilac from his cap and thrusts it out as he passes. 'Souvenir!' he says, lightly, and the young woman catches the blossom and draws herself up with her eyes sparkling and calls, 'Bonne chance, Messieurs. Goo-o-o-d lock.' She repeats the words over and over while the regiment passes, and the men answer, 'Bong chawnse' and 'Good luck,' and such scraps of French as they know--or think they know. The women stand in the sunshine and watch them long after they have passed, and then turn slowly and move on to their church and their prayers.

The regiment tramps on. It moves with the assured stamp and swing of men who know themselves and know their game, and have confidence in their strength and fitness. Their clothes are faded and weather-stained, their belts and straps and equipments chafed and worn, the woodwork of their rifles smooth of butt and shiny of hand-grip from much using and cleaning. Their faces bronzed and weather-beaten, and with a dew of perspiration just damping their foreheads--where men less fit would be streaming sweat--are full-cheeked and glowing with health, and cheek and chin razored clean and smooth as a guardsman's going on church parade. The whole regiment looks fresh and well set-up and clean-cut, satisfied with the day and not bothering about the morrow, magnificently strong and healthy, carelessly content and happy, not anxious to go out of its way to find a fight, but impossible to move aside from its way by the fight that does find it--all of which is to say it looks exactly what it is, a British regiment of the regular Line, war-hardened by eight or nine months' fighting, moving up from a four days' rest back into the firing line.

It is fairly early in the day, and the sun, although it is bright enough to bring out the full colour of the green grass and trees, the yellow laburnum, and the purple lilac, is not hot enough to make marching uncomfortable. The road, a main route between two towns, is paved with flat cobbles about the size of large bricks, and bordered mile after mile with tall poplars. There are farms and hamlets and villages strung close along the road, and round and about all these houses are women and children, and many men in khaki, a few dogs, some pigs perhaps, and near the farms plenty of poultry. By most of the farms, too, are orchards and fruit-trees in blossom; and in some of these lines of horses are ranked or wagons are parked, sheltered by the trees from aerial observation. For all this, it must be remembered, is far enough back from the firing line to be beyond the reach of any but the longest-range guns--guns so big that they are not likely to waste some tons of shells on the off-chance of hitting an encampment and disabling few or many horses or wagons.

Towards noon the regiment swings off the road and halts in a large orchard; rifles are stood aside, equipments and packs are thrown off, tunics unbuttoned and flung open or off, and the men drop with puffing sighs of satisfaction on the springy turf under the shade of the fruit-trees. The 'travelling cookers' rumble up and huge cauldrons of stew and potatoes are slung off, carried to the different companies, and served steaming hot to the hungry men. A boon among boons these same cookers, less so perhaps now that the warmer weather is here, but a blessing beyond price in the bitter cold and constant wet of the past winter, when a hot meal served without waiting kept heart in many men and even life itself in some. Their fires were lit before the regiment broke camp this morning, and the dinners have been jolting over the long miles since sun-up, cooking as comfortably and well as they would in the best-appointed camp or barrack cook-house.

The men eat mightily, then light their pipes and cigarettes and loll at their ease. The trees are masses of clustering pink and white blossom, the grass is carpeted thick with the white of fallen petals and splashed with sunlight and shade. A few slow-moving clouds drift lazily across the blue sky, the big, fat bees drone their sleepy song amongst the blossoms, the birds rustle and twitter amongst the leaves and flit from bough to bough. It would be hard to find a more peaceful picture in any country steeped in the most profound peace. There is not one jarring note-- until the 'honk, honk' of a motor is followed by the breathless, panting whirr of the engine, and a big car flashes down the road and past, travelling at the topmost of its top speed. There is just time to glimpse the khaki hood and the thick scarlet cross blazing on a white circle, and the car is gone. Empty as it is, it is moving fast, and with luck and a clear road it will be well inside the danger zone at the back door of the trenches in less than twenty minutes. In half an hour perhaps it will have picked up its full load, and be sliding back smoothly and gently down the cobbled road, swinging carefully now to this side to avoid some scattered bricks, now to that to dodge a shell-hole patched with gravel, driven down as tenderly and gently as it was driven up fiercely and recklessly.

Presently there are a few quiet orders, a few minutes' stir and movement, a shifting to and fro of khaki against the green and pink and white . . . and the com-panies have fallen in and stand in straight rulered ranks. A pause, a sharp order or two, and the quick staccato of 'numbering off' ripples swiftly down the lines; an-other pause, another order, the long ranks blur and melt, harden and halt instantly in a new shape; and evenly and steadily the ranked fours swing off, turn out into the road, and go tramping down between the poplars. There has been no flurry, no hustle, no confusion. The whole thing has moved with the smoothness and precision and effortless ease of a properly adjusted, well-oiled machine--which, after all, is just what the regiment is. The pace is apparently leisurely, or even lazy, but it eats up the miles amazingly, and it can be kept up with the shortest of halts from dawn to dusk.

As the miles unwind behind the regiment the character of the country begins to change. There are fewer women and children to be seen now; there are more roofless buildings, more house-fronts gaping doorless and windowless, more walls with ragged rents, and tumbled heaps of brick lying under the yawning black holes. But the grass is still green, and the trees thick with foliage, the fields neatly ploughed and tilled and cultivated, with here and there a staring notice planted on the edge of a field, where the long, straight drills are sprinkled with budding green--'Crops sown. Do not walk here.' Altogether there is little sign of the heavy hand of war upon the country, and such signs as there are remain unobtrusive and wrapped up in springing verdure and bloom and blossom. Even the trapping of war, the fighting machine itself, wears a holiday or--at most--an Easter-peace-manoeuvre appearance. A heavy battery has its guns so carefully concealed, so bowered in green, that it is only the presence of the lounging gunners and close, searching looks that reveal a few inches of muzzle peering out towards the hill crest in front. Scattered about behind the guns, covered with beautiful green turf, shadowed by growing trees, are the dwelling-places of the gunners, deep 'dug-outs,' with no visible sign of their existence except the square, black hole of the doorway. Out in the open a man sits with a pair of field-glasses, sweeping the sky. He is the aeroplane look-out, and at the first sign of a distant speck in the sky or the drone of an engine he blows shrilly on his whistle; every man dives to earth or under cover, and remains motionless until the whistle signals all clear again. An enemy aeroplane might drop to within pistol shot and search for an hour without finding a sign of the battery.

When the regiment swerves off the main road and moves down a winding side-track over open fields, past tree-encircled farms, and along by thick-leaved hedges, it passes more of these Jack-in-the-Green concealed batteries. All wear the same look of happy and indolent ease. Near one is a stream, and the gunners are bathing in an artificially made pool, plunging and splashing in showers of glistening drops. They are like school boys at a picnic. It seems utterly ridiculous to think that they are grim fighting men whose business in life for months past and for months to come is to kill and kill, and to be killed themselves if such is the fortune of war. Another battery of field artillery passes on the road. But even here, shorn of their concealing greenery, in all the bare working-and-ready-for-business apparel of 'marching order,' there is little to suggest real war. Drivers and gunners are spruce and neat and clean, the horses are sleek and well fed and groomed till their skins shine like satin in the sun, the harness is polished and speckless, bits and stirrup-irons and chains and all the scraps of steel and brass twinkle and wink in bright and shining splendour. The ropes of the traces--the last touch of pride in perfection this, surely--are scrubbed and whitened. The whole battery is as spick and span, as complete and immaculate, as if it were waiting to walk into the arena at the Naval and Military Tournament. Such scrupulous perfection on active service sounds perhaps unnecessary or even extravagant. But the teams, remember, have been for weeks past luxuriating in comfortable ease miles back in their 'wagon-line' billets, where the horses have done nothing for days on end but feed and grow fat, and the drivers nothing but clean up and look after their teams and harness. If the guns up in the firing line had to shift position it has meant no more to the teams than a break of the monotony for a day or two, a night or two's marching, and a return to the rear.

It is afternoon now, and the regiment is drawing near to the trenches. The slanting sun begins to throw long shadows from the poplars. The open fields are covered with tall grass and hay that moves in long, slow, undulating waves under the gentle breeze that is rising. The sloping light falling on them gives the waves an extraordinary resemblance to the lazy swell on a summer sea. Here and there the fields are splashed with broad bands of vivid colour--the blazing scarlet of poppies, the glowing cloth-of-gold of yellow mustard, the rich, deep, splendid blue of corn-flowers.

For one or two miles past the track has been plainly marked by sign-posts bearing directions to the various trenches and their entrances. Now, at a parting of the main track, a group of 'guides'--men from the regiment being relieved from the trenches--wait the incoming regiment. Company by company, platoon by platoon, the regiment moves off to the appointed places, and by company and platoon the outcoming regiment gathers up its belongings and moves out. In most parts of the firing line these changes would only be made after dark. But this section bears the reputation of being a 'peaceful' one, the Germans opposite of being 'tame,' so the reliefs are made in daytime, more or less in safety. There has been no serious fighting here for months. Constant sniping and bickering between the forward firing trenches has, of course, always gone on, but there has been no attack one way or the other, little shell-fire, and few aeroplanes over.

The companies that 'take over' the support trenches get varied instructions and advice about tending the plants and flowers round the dugouts, and watering the mustard-and-cress box. They absorb the advice, strip their accoutrements and tunics, roll up their shirt-sleeves, and open the throats, fish out soap and towels from their packs, and proceed to the pump to lather and wash copiously. The companies for the forward trench march down interminable communication trenches, distribute themselves along the parapet, and also absorb advice from the outgoing tenants--advice of the positions of enemy snipers, the hours when activity and when peace may be expected, the specially 'unhealthy' spots where a sniper's bullet or a bomb must be watched for, the angles and loopholes that give the best look-out. The trenches are deep and well-made, the parapets solidly constructed. For four days or six, or as many as the regiment remains 'in,' the range of the men's vision will be the walls of the trench, the piled sandbags, the inside of their dug-outs, and a view (taken in peeps through a loophole or reflected in a periscope mirror) of about fifty to a hundred yards of 'neutral ground' and the German parapet beyond. The neutral ground is covered with a jungle of coarse grass, edged on both sides with a tangle of barbed wire.

Close to the German parapet are a few black, huddled heaps--dead Germans, shot down while out in a working party on the wire at night, and left there to rot, and some killed in their own trench, and tumbled out over the parapet by their own comrades. The drowsy silence is broken at long intervals by a rifle shot; a lark pours out a stream of joyful thrilling song.

*   *   *   *   *

A mile or two back from the firing line a couple of big motor-cars swing over the crest of a gentle rise, swoop down into the dip, and halt suddenly. A little group of men with scarlet staff-bands on their caps and tabs on their collars climb out of the cars and move off the track into the grass of the hollow. They prod sticks at the ground, stamp on it, dig a heel in, to test its hardness and dryness.

The General looks round. 'This is about as low-lying a spot as we have on this part of front,' he says to his Chief of Staff. 'If it is dry enough here it must be dry enough everywhere else.'

The Chief assents, and for a space the group stands looking round the sunlit fields and up at the clear sky. But their thoughts are not of the beauties of the peaceful landscape. The words of the General are the key to all their thoughts. For them the promise of spring is a grim and a sinister thing; to them the springy green turf carpet on the fields means ground fit to bear the weight of teams and guns, dry enough to give firm foothold to the ranks of infantry charging across the death-trap of the neutral ground, where clogging, wet, slippery mud adds to the minutes under the hail of fire and every minute there in the open means hundreds of lives lost. The hard, dry road underfoot means merely that roads are passable for heavy guns and transport. The thick green foliage of the trees is so much cover for guns and the moving of troops and transport under concealment from air observation; the clear, blue sky promises the continuance of fine weather, the final release from the inactivity of the trenches. To these men the 'Promise of Spring' is the promise of the crescendo of battle and slaughter.

The General and his Staff are standing in the middle of a wide patch of poppies, spread out in a bright scarlet that matches exactly the red splashes on the brows and throats of the group. They move slowly back towards the cars, and as they walk the red ripples and swirls against their boots and about their knees.

One might imagine them wading knee-deep in a river of blood.

THE ADVANCE

'The attack has resulted in our line being advanced from one to two hundred yards along a front of over one thousand yards.'--OFFICIAL DESPATCH.

Down to the rawest hand in the latest-joined drafts, everyone knew for a week before the attack commenced that 'something was on,' and for twenty-four hours before that the 'something' was a move of some importance, no mere affair of a battalion or two, or even of brigades, but of divisions and corps and armies. There had been vague stirrings in the regiments far behind the firing line 'in rest,' refittings and completings of kits, reissuing of worn equipments, and a most ominous anxiety that each man was duly equipped with an 'identity disc,' the tell-tale little badge that hangs always round the neck of a man on active service and that bears the word of who he is when he is brought in wounded--who he was when brought in dead. The old hands judged all the signs correctly and summed them up in a sentence, 'Being fattened for the slaughter,' and were in no degree surprised when the sudden order came to move. Those farthest back moved up the first stages by daylight, but when they came within reach of the rumbling guns they were halted and bivouacked to wait for night to cloak their movements from the prying eyes of the enemy 'planes. The enemy might have--probably had--an inkling of the coming attack; but they might not know exactly the portion of front selected for the heaviest pressure, and this must be kept secret till the last possible moment. So the final filing up into the forward and support trenches was done by night, and was so complete by daylight that no sign of unwonted movement could be discerned from the enemy trenches and observing stations when day broke.

It was a beautiful morning--soft and mildly warm and sunny, with just a slight haze hanging low to tone the growing light, and, incidentally, to delay the opening of fire from the guns. Anyone standing midway between the forward firing trenches might have looked in vain for living sign of the massed hordes waiting the word to be at each other's throats. Looking forward from behind the British lines, it could be seen that the trenches and parapets were packed with men; but no man showed head over parapet, and, seen from the enemy's side, the parapets presented blank, lifeless walls, the trenches gave no glimpse of life. All the bustle and movement of the night before was finished. At midnight every road and track leading to the forward trenches had been brimming with men, with regiments tramping slowly or squatting stolidly by the roadside, smoking much and talking little, had been crawling with transport, with ammunition carts, and ambulances and stretcher-parties, and sappers heavily laden with sandbags and rolls of barbed wire. The trenches--support, communication, and firing--had trickled with creeping rivulets of khaki caps and been a-bristle with bobbing rifle-barrels. Further back amongst the lines of guns the last loads of ammunition were rumbling up to the batteries, the last shells required to 'complete establishment'--and over-complete it--were being stowed in safe proximity to the guns. At midnight there were scores of thousands of men and animals busily at work with preparations for the slaughter-pen of the morrow. Before midnight came again the bustle would be renewed, and the circling ripples of activity would be spreading and widening from the central splash of the battle front till the last waves washed back to Berlin and London, brimming the hospitals and swirling through the munition factories. But now at daybreak the battle-field was steeped in brooding calm. Across the open space of the neutral ground a few trench periscopes peered anxiously for any sign of movement, and saw none; the batteries' 'forward observing officers,' tucked away in carefully chosen and hidden look-outs, fidgeted with wrist-watches and field-glasses, and passed back by telephone continual messages about the strength of the growing light and the lifting haze. An aeroplane droned high overhead, and an 'Archibald' (anti-aircraft gun) or two began to pattern the sky about it with a trail of fleecy white smoke-puffs. The 'plane sailed on and out of sight, the smoke-puffs and the wheezy barks of 'Archibald' receding after it. Another period of silence followed. It was broken by a faint report like the sound of a far-off door being slammed, and almost at the same instant there came to the ear the faint thin whistle of an approaching shell. The whistle rose to a rush and a roar that cut off abruptly in a thunderous bang. The shell pitched harmlessly on the open ground between the forward and support trenches. Again came that faint 'slam,' this time repeated by four, and the 'bouquet' of four shells crumped down almost on top of the support line. The four crashes might have been a signal to the British guns. About a dozen reports thudded out quickly and separately, and then in one terrific blast of sound the whole line broke out in heavy fire. The infantry in the trenches could distinguish the quick-following bangs of the guns directly in line behind them, could separate the vicious swish and rush of the shells passing immediately over their heads. Apart from these, the reports blent in one long throbbing pulse of noise, an indescribable medley of moanings, shrieks, and whistling in the air rent by the passing shells. So ear-filling and confused was the clamour that the first sharp, sudden bursts of the enemy shells over our trenches were taken by the infantry for their own artillery's shells falling short; but a very few moments proved plainly enough that the enemy were replying vigorously to our fire. They had the ranges well marked, too, and huge rents began to show in our parapets, strings of casualties began to trickle back to the dressing stations in a stream that was to flow steady and unbroken for many days and nights. But the enemy defences showed more and quicker signs of damage, especially at the main points, where the massed guns were busy breaching the selected spots. Here the lighter guns were pouring a hurricane of shrapnel on the dense thickets of barbed-wire entanglements piled in loose loops and coils, strung in a criss-cross network between pegs and stakes along the edge of the neutral ground; the howitzers and heavies were pounding and hammering at the parapets and the communication trenches beyond.

For half an hour the appalling uproar continued, the solid earth shook to the roar of the guns and the crashing of the shells. By the end of that time both fronts to a depth of hundreds of yards were shrouded in a slow-drifting haze of smoke and dust, through which the flashes of the bursting shell blazed in quick glares of vivid light, and the spots of their falling were marked by gushes of smoke and upflung billowing clouds of thick dust. So far the noise was only and all of guns and shell fire, but now from far out on one of the flanks a new note began to weave itself into the uproar--the sharper crackle and clatter of rifle and machine-gun fire.

Along the line of front marked for the main assault the guns suddenly lifted their fire and commenced to pour it down further back, although a number of the lighter guns continued to sweep the front parapet with gusts of shrapnel. And then suddenly it could be seen that the front British trench was alive and astir. The infantry, who had been crouched and prone in the shelter of their trenches, rose suddenly and began to clamber over the parapets into the open and make their way out through the maze of their own entanglements. Instantly the parapet opposite began to crackle with rifle fire and to beat out a steady tattoo from the hammering machine-guns. The bullets hissed and spat across the open and hailed upon the opposite parapet. Scores, hundreds of men fell before they could clear the entanglements to form up in the open, dropped as they climbed the parapet, or even as they stood up and raised a head above it. But the mass poured out, shook itself roughly into line, and began to run across the open. They ran for the most part with shoulders hunched and heads stooped, as men would run through a heavy rainstorm to a near shelter And as they ran they stumbled and fell and picked themselves up and ran again--or crumpled up and lay still or squirming feebly. As the line swept on doggedly it thinned and shredded into broken groups. The men dropped under the rifle bullets, singly or in twos and threes; the bursting shells tore great gaps in the line, snatching a dozen men at a mouthful; here and there, where it ran into the effective sweep of a maxim, the line simply withered and dropped and stayed still in a string of huddled heaps amongst and on which the bullets continued to drum and thud. The open ground was a full hundred yards across at the widest point where the main attack was delivering. Fifty yards across, the battalion assaulting was no longer a line, but a scattered series of groups like beads on a broken string; sixty yards across and the groups had dwindled to single men and couples with desperately long intervals between; seventy yards, and there were no more than odd occasional men, with one little bunch near the centre that had by some extraordinary chance escaped the sleet of bullets; at eighty yards a sudden swirl of lead caught this last group--and the line at last was gone, wiped out, the open was swept clear of those dogged runners. The open ground was dotted thick with men, men lying prone and still, men crawling on hands and knees, men dragging themselves slowly and painfully with trailing, useless legs, men limping, hobbling, staggering, in a desperate endeavour to get back to their parapet and escape the bullets and shrapnel that still stormed down upon them. The British gunners dropped their ranges again, and a deluge of shells and shrapnel burst crashing and whistling upon the enemy's front parapet. The rifle fire slackened and almost died, and the last survivors of the charge had such chance as was left by the enemy's shells to reach the shelter of their trench. Groups of stretcher-bearers leaped out over the parapet and ran to pick up the wounded, and hard on their heels another line of infantry swarmed out and formed up for another attack. As they went forward at a run the roar of rifles and machine-guns swelled again, and the hail of bullets began to sweep across to meet them. Into the forward trench they had vacated, the stream of another battalion poured, and had commenced to climb out in their turn before the advancing line was much more than half-way across. This time the casualties, although appallingly heavy, were not so hopelessly severe as in the first charge, probably because a salient of the enemy trench to a flank had been reached by a battalion farther along, and the devastating enfilading fire of rifles and machine-guns cut off. This time the broken remnants of the line reached the barbed wires, gathered in little knots as the individual men ran up and down along the face of the entanglements looking for the lanes cut clearest by the sweeping shrapnel, streamed through with men still falling at every step, reached the parapet and leaped over and down. The guns had held their fire on the trench till the last possible moment, and now they lifted again and sought to drop across the further lines and the communication trenches a shrapnel 'curtain' through which no reinforcements could pass and live. The following battalion came surging across, losing heavily, but still bearing weight enough to tell when at last they poured in over the parapet.

The neutral ground, the deadly open and exposed space, was won. It had been crossed at other points, and now it only remained to see if the hold could be maintained and strengthened and extended.

The fighting fell to a new phase--the work of the short-arm bayonet thrust and the bomb-throwers. In the gaps between the points where the trench was taken the enemy fought with the desperation of trapped rats. The trench had to be taken traverse by traverse. The bombers lobbed their missiles over into the traverse ahead of them in showers, and immediately the explosions crashed out, swung round the corner with a rush to be met in turn with bullets or bursting bombs. Sometimes a space of two or three traverses was blasted bare of life and rendered untenable for long minutes on end by a constant succession of grenades and bombs. In places, the men of one side or the other leaped up out of the trench, risking the bullets that sleeted across the level ground, and emptied a clip of cartridges or hurled half a dozen grenades down into the trench further along. But for the most part the fight raged below ground-level, at times even below the level of the trench floor, where a handful of men held out in a deep dug-out. If the entrance could be reached, a few bombs speedily settled the affair; but where the defenders had hastily blocked themselves in with a barricade of sandbags or planks, so that grenades could not be pitched in, there was nothing left to do but crowd in against the rifle muzzles that poked out and spurted bullets from the openings, tear down the defences, and so come at the defenders. And all the time the captured trench was pelted by shells-- high-explosive and shrapnel. At the entrances of the communication trenches that led back to the support trenches the fiercest fighting raged continually, with men struggling to block the path with sandbags and others striving to tear them down, while on both sides their fellows fought over them with bayonet and butt. In more than one such place the barricade was at last built by the heap of the dead who had fought for possession; in others, crude barriers of earth and sandbags were piled up and fought across and pulled down and built up again a dozen times.

In the middle of the ferocious individual hand-to-hand fighting a counter-at- tack was launched against the captured trench. A swarm of the enemy leaped from the next trench and rushed across the twenty or thirty yards of open to the captured front line. But the counterattack had been expected. The guns caught the attack- ers as they left their trench and beat them down in scores. A line of riflemen had been installed under cover of what had been the parapet of the enemy front trench, and this line broke out in 'the mad minute' of rifle fire. The shrapnel and the rifles between them smashed the counter-attack before it had well formed. It was cut down in swathes and had totally collapsed before it reached half-way to the cap- tured trench. But another was hurled forward instantly, was up out of the trench and streaming across the open before the infantry had finished re-charging their magazines. Then the rifles spoke again in rolling crashes, the screaming shrapnel pounced again on the trench that still erupted hurrying men, while from the cap- tured trench itself came hurtling bombs and grenades. Smoke and dust leaped and swirled in dense clouds about the trenches and the open between them, but through the haze the ragged front fringe of the attack loomed suddenly and pressed on to the very lip of the trench. Beyond that point it appeared it could not pass. The British infantry, cramming full cartridge-clips into their magazines, poured a fresh cataract of lead across the broken parapet into the charging ranks, and the ranks shivered and stopped and melted away beneath the fire, while the remnants broke and fled back to cover. With a yell the defenders of a moment before became the attackers. They leaped the trench and fell with the bayonet on the flying survivors of the counter-attack. For the most part these were killed as they fled; but here and there groups of them turned at bay, and in a dozen places as many fights raged bitterly for a few minutes, while the fresh attack pushed on to the next trench. A withering fire poured from it but could not stop the rush that fought its way on and into the second-line trench. From now the front lost connection or cohesion. Here and there the attackers broke in on the second line, exterminated that portion of the defence in its path or was itself exterminated there. Where it won footing it spread raging to either side along the trench, shooting, stabbing, flinging hand grenades and bearing down the defenders by the sheer fury of the attack. The movement spread along the line, and with a sudden leap and rush the second line was gained along a front of nearly a mile. In parts this attack overshot its mark, broke through and over the second line and, tearing and hacking through a network of wire, into the third trench. In part the second line still held out; and even after it was all completely taken, the communication trenches between the first and second line were filled with combatants who fought on furiously, heedless of whether friend or foe held trench to front or rear, intent only on the business at their own bayonet points, to kill the enemy facing them and push in and kill the ones behind. Fresh supports pressed into the captured positions, and, backed by their weight, the attack surged on again in a fresh spasm of fury. It secured foothold in great sections of the third line, and even, without waiting to see the whole of it made good, attempted to rush the fourth line. At one or two points the gallant attempt succeeded, and a handful of men hung on desperately for some hours, their further advance impossible, their retreat, had they attempted it, almost equally so, cut off from reinforcements, short of ammunition, and entirely without bombs or grenades. When their ammunition was expended they used rifles and cartridges taken from the enemy dead in the trench; having no grenades they snatched and hurled back on the instant any that fell with fuses still burning. They waged their unequal fight to the last minute and were killed out to the last man.

The third line was not completely held or even taken. One or two loopholed and machine-gunned dug-out redoubts, or 'keeps,' held out strenuously, and before they could be reduced--entrance being gained at last literally by tearing the place down sandbag by sandbag till a hole was made and grenade after grenade flung in--other parts of the trench had been recaptured. The weak point that so often hampers attack was making itself felt. The bombers and 'grenadiers' had exhausted the stock they carried; fresh supplies were scanty, were brought up with difficulty, and distributed to the most urgently required places with still greater difficulty. The ammunition carriers had to cross the open of the old neutral ground, the battered first trench, pass along communication trenches choked with dead and wounded, or again cross the open to the second and third line. All the time they were under the fire of high-explosive shells and had to pass through a zone or 'barrage' of shrapnel built across their path for just this special purpose of destroying supports and supplies. Our own artillery were playing exactly the same game behind the enemy lines, but in these lines were ample stores of cartridges and grenades, bombs, and trench-mortars. The third and fourth lines were within easy bomb- and grenade-throwing distance, and were connected by numerous passage-ways. On this front the contest became a bombing duel, and because the British were woefully short of bombs and the enemy could throw five to their one, they were once again 'bombed out' and forced to retire. But by now the second trench had been put in some state of defence towards its new front, and here the British line stayed fast and set its teeth and doggedly endured the torment of the bombs and the destruction of the pounding shells. Without rest or respite they endured till night, and on through the night, under the glare of flares and the long-drawn punishment of the shell fire, until the following day brought with the dawn fresh supports for a renewal of the struggle. The battered fragments of the first attacking battalions were withdrawn, often with corporals for company leaders, and lieutenants or captains commanding battalions whose full remaining strength would hardly make a company. The battle might only have been well begun, but at least, thanks to them and to those scattered heaps lying among the grass, spread in clumps and circles about the yawning shell-holes, buried beneath the broken parapets and in the smashed trenches--to them, and those, and these others passing out with haggard, pain-lined faces, shattered limbs, and torn bodies on the red, wet stretchers to the dressing stations, at least, the battle was well begun. The sappers were hard at work in the darkness consolidating the captured positions, and these would surely now be held firm. Whatever was to follow, these first regiments had done their share.

Two lines of trenches were taken; the line was advanced--advanced, it is true, a bare one or two hundred yards, but with lives poured out like water over each foot of the advance, with every inch of the ground gained marking a well-spring and fountain-head of a river of pain, of a suffering beyond all words, of a glory above and beyond all suffering.

A CONVERT TO CONSCRIPTION

'. . . have maintained and consolidated our position in the captured trench.'--EXTRACT FROM OFFICIAL DESPATCH.

Number nine-two-ought-three-six, Sapper Duffy, J., 'A' Section, Southland Company, Royal Engineers, had been before the War plain Jem Duffy, labourer, and as such had been an ardent anti-militarist, anti-conscriptionist, and anti-everything else his labour leaders and agitators told him. His anti-militarist beliefs were sunk soon after the beginning of the War, and there is almost a complete story itself in the tale of their sinking, weighted first by a girl, who looked ahead no further than the pleasure of walking out with a khaki uniform, and finally plunged into the deeps of the Army by the gibe of a stauncher anti-militarist during a heated argument that, 'if he believed now in fighting, why didn't he go'n fight himself?' But even after his enlistment he remained true to his beliefs in voluntary service, and the account of his conversion to the principles of Conscription--no half-and-half measures of 'military training' or rifle clubs or hybrid arrangements of that sort, but out-and-out Conscription--may be more interesting, as it certainly is more typical, of the conversion of more thousands of members of the Serving Forces than will ever be known--until those same thousands return to their civilian lives and the holding of their civilian votes.

*　　*　　*　　*　　*

By nightfall the captured trench--well, it was only a courtesy title to call it a trench. Previous to the assault, the British guns had knocked it about a good deal, bombs and grenades had helped further to disrupt it in the attacks and counter-attacks during the day, and finally, after it was captured and held, the enemy had shelled and high-explosived it out of any likeness to a real trench. But the infantry had clung throughout the day to the ruins, had beaten off several strong counter-attacks, and in the intervals had done what they could to dig themselves more securely in and re-pile some heaps of sandbags from the shattered parapet on the trench's new front. The casualties had been heavy, and since there was no passage from the front British trench to the captured portion of the German except across the open of the 'neutral' ground, most of the wounded and all the killed had had to remain under such cover as could be found in the wrecked trench. The position of the unwounded was bad enough and unpleasant enough, but it was a great deal worse for the wounded. A bad wound damages mentally as well as physically. The 'casualty' is out of the fight, has had a first field dressing placed on his wound, has been set on one side to be removed at the first opportunity to the dressing station and the rear. He can do nothing more to protect himself or take such cover as of-fers. He is in the hands of the stretcher-bearers and must submit to be moved when and where they think fit. And in this case the casualties did not even have the satisfaction of knowing that every minute that passed meant a minute farther from the danger zone, a minute nearer to safety and to the doctors, and the hospitals' hope of healing. Here they had to be throughout the long day, hearing the shriek of each approaching shell, waiting for the crash of its fall, wondering each time if ***this*** one, the rush of its approach rising louder and louder to an appalling screech, was going to be the finish--a 'direct hit.' Many of the wounded were wounded again, or killed as they lay; and from others the strength and the life had drained slowly out before nightfall. But now that darkness had come the casualties moved out and the supports moved in. From what had been the German second trench, and on this portion of front was now their forward one, lights were continually going up and bursts of rifle and machine-gun fire were coming; and an occasional shell still whooped up and burst over or behind the captured trench. This meant that the men--supports, and food and water carriers, and stretcher-bearers--were under a dangerous fire even at night in crossing the old 'neutral' ground, and it meant that one of the first jobs absolutely necessary to the holding of the captured trench was the making of a connecting path more or less safe for moving men, ammunition, and food by night or day.

This, then, was the position of affairs when 'A' section of the Southland Company of Engineers came up to take a hand, and this communication trench was the task that Sapper Duffy, J., found himself set to work on. Personally Sapper Duffy knew nothing of, and cared less for, the tactical situation. All he knew or cared about was that he had done a longish march up from the rear the night before, that he had put in a hard day's work carrying up bales of sandbags and rolls of barbed wire from the carts to the trenches, and that here before him was another night's hard labour, to say nothing of the prospect of being drilled by a rifle bullet or mangled by a shell. All the information given him and his section by their section officer was that they were to dig a communication trench, that it must be completed before morning, that as long as they were above-ground they would probably be under a nasty fire, and that therefore the sooner they dug themselves down under cover the better it would be for the job and for all concerned. 'A' section removed its equipment and tunics and moved out on to the 'neutral' ground in its shirt-sleeves, shivering at first in the raw cold and at the touch of the drizzling rain, but knowing that the work would very soon warm them beyond need of hampering clothes. In the ordinary course, digging a trench under fire is done more or less under cover by sapping-- digging the first part in a covered spot, standing in the deep hole, cutting down the 'face' and gradually burrowing a way across the danger zone. The advantage of this method is that the workers keep digging their way forward while all the time they are below ground and in the safety of the sap they dig. The disadvantage is that the narrow trench only allows one or two men to get at its end or 'face' to dig, and the work consequently takes time. Here it was urgent that the work be completed that night, because it was very certain that as soon as its whereabouts was disclosed by daylight it would be subjected to a fire too severe to allow any party to work, even if the necessary passage of men to and fro would leave any room for a working party.

The digging therefore had to be done down from the surface, and the diggers, until they had sunk themselves into safety, had to stand and work fully exposed to the bullets that whined and hissed across from the enemy trenches.

A zigzag line had been laid down to mark the track of the trench, and Sapper Duffy was placed by his sergeant on this line and told briefly to 'get on with it.' Sapper Duffy spat on his hands, placed his spade on the exact spot indicated, drove it down, and began to dig at a rate that was apparently leisurely but actually was methodical and nicely calculated to a speed that could be long and unbrokenly sustained. During the first minute many bullets whistled and sang past, and Sapper Duffy took no notice. A couple went 'whutt' past his ear, and he swore and slightly increased his working speed. When a bullet whistles or sings past, it is a comfortable distance clear; when it goes 'hiss' or 'swish,' it is too close for safety; and when it says 'whutt' very sharply and viciously, it is merely a matter of being a few inches out either way. Sapper Duffy had learned all this by full experience, and now the number of 'whutts' he heard gave him a very clear understanding of the dangers of this particular job. He was the farthest out man of the line. On his left hand he could just distinguish the dim figure of another digger, stooping and straightening, stooping and straightening, with the rhythm and regularity of a machine. On his right hand was empty darkness, lit up every now and then by the glow of a flare-light showing indistinctly through the drizzling rain. Out of the darkness, or looming big against the misty light, figures came and went stumbling and slipping in the mud--stretcher-bearers carrying or supporting the wounded, a ration party staggering under boxes balanced on shoulders, a strung-out line of supports stooped and trying to move quietly, men in double files linked together by swinging ammunition boxes. All these things Sapper Duffy saw out of the tail of his eye, and without stopping or slacking the pace of his digging. He fell unconsciously to timing his movements to those of the other man, and for a time the machine became a twin-engine working beat for beat--thrust, stoop, straighten, heave; thrust, stoop, straighten, heave. Then a bullet said the indescribable word that means 'hit' and Duffy found that the other half of the machine had stopped suddenly and collapsed in a little heap. Somewhere along the line a voice called softly 'Stretcher-bearers,' and almost on the word two men and a stretcher materialised out of the darkness and a third was stooping over the broken machine. 'He's gone,' said the third man after a pause. 'Lift him clear.' The two men dropped the stretcher, stooped and fumbled, lifted the limp figure, laid it down a few yards away from the line, and vanished in the direction of another call. Sapper Duffy was alone with his spade and a foot-deep square hole--and the hissing bullets. The thoughts of the dead man so close beside him disturbed him vaguely, although he had never given a thought to the scores of dead he had seen behind the trench and that he knew were scattered thick over the 'neutral' ground where they had fallen in the first charge. But this man had been one of his own company and his own section--it was different about him somehow. Yet of course Sapper Duffy knew that the dead must at times lie where they fall, because the living must always come before the dead, especially while there are many more wounded than there are stretchers or stretcher-bearers. But all the same he didn't like poor old 'Jigger' Adams being left there--didn't see how he could go home and face old 'Jigger's' missus and tell her he'd come away and left 'Jigger' lying in the mud of a mangel-wurzel field. Blest if he wouldn't have a try when they were going to give Jigger a lift back. A line of men, shirt-sleeved like himself and carrying spades in their hands, moved out past him. An officer led them, and another with Sapper Duffy's section officer brought up the rear, and passed along the word to halt when he reached Daffy. 'Here's the outside man of my lot,' he said, 'so you'll join on beyond him. You've just come in, I hear, so I suppose your men are fresh?'

'Fresh!' said the other disgustedly. 'Not much. They've been digging trenches all day about four miles back. It's too sickening. Pity we don't do like the Boches--conscript all the able-bodied civilians and make 'em do all this trench-digging in rear. Then we might be fresh for the firing line.'

'Tut, tut--mustn't talk about conscripting 'em,' said Duffy's officer reprovingly. 'One volunteer, y'know--worth ten pressed men.'

'Yes,' said the other, 'but when there isn't enough of the "one volunteer" it's about time to collar the ten pressed.'

Two or three flares went up almost simultaneously from the enemy's line, the crackle of fire rose to a brisk fusillade, and through it ran the sharp 'rat-at-at-at' of a machine-gun. The rising sound of the reports told plainly of the swinging muzzle, and officers and men dropped flat in the mud and waited till the sweeping bullets had passed over their heads. Men may work on and 'chance it' against rifle fire alone, but the sweep of a machine-gun is beyond chance, and very near to the certainty of sudden death to all in the circle of its swing.

The officers passed on and the new men began to dig. Sapper Duffy also re-sumed work, and as he did so he noticed there was something familiar about the bulky shape of the new digger next to him.

'What lot are you?' asked the new man, heaving out the first spadeful rapidly and dexterously.

'We're 'A' Section, Southland Company,' said Duffy, 'an' I say--ain't you Beefy Wilson?'

'That's me,' said the other without checking his spade. 'And blow me! you must be Duffy--Jem Duffy.'

'That's right,' said Duffy. 'But I didn't know you'd joined, Beefy.'

'Just a week or two after you,' said Beefy.

'Didjer know boss's two sons had got commissions? Joined the Sappers an' tried to raise a company out o' the works to join. Couldn't though. I was the only one.'

'Look out--'ere's that blanky maxim again,' said Duffy, and they dropped flat very hurriedly.

There was no more conversation at the moment. There were too many bullets about to encourage any lingering there, and both men wanted all their breath for their work. It was hard work too. Duffy's back and shoulder and arm muscles began to ache dully, but he stuck doggedly to it. He even made an attempt to speed up to Beefy's rate of shovelling, although he knew by old experience alongside Beefy that he could never keep up with him, the unchallenged champion of the old gang.

Whether it was that the lifting rain had made them more visible or that the sound of their digging had been heard they never knew, but the rifle fire for some reason became faster and closer, and again and again the call passed for stretcher-bearers, and a constant stream of wounded began to trickle back from the trench-diggers. Duffy's section was not so badly off now because they had sunk themselves hip deep, and the earth they threw out in a parapet gave extra protection. But it was harder work for them now because they stood in soft mud and water well above the ankles. The new company, being the more exposed, suffered more from the fire; but each man of them had a smaller portion of trench to dig, so they were catching up on the first workers. But all spaded furiously and in haste to be done with the job, while the officers and sergeants moved up and down the line and watched the progress made.

More cold-bloodedly unpleasant work it would be hard to imagine. The men had none of the thrill and heat of combat to help them; they had not the hope that a man has in a charge across the open--that a minute or two gets the worst of it over; they had not even the chance the fighting man has where at least his hand may save his head. Their business was to stand in the one spot, open and unprotected, and without hope of cover or protection for a good hour or more on end. They must pay no heed to the singing bullets, to the crash of a bursting shell, to the rising and falling glow of the flares. Simply they must give body and mind to the job in hand, and dig and dig and keep on digging. There had been many brave deeds done by the fighting men on that day: there had been bold leading and bold following in the first rush across the open against a tornado of fire; there had been forlorn-hope dashes for ammunition or to pick up wounded; there had been dogged and desperate courage in clinging all day to the battered trench under an earth-shaking tempest of high-explosive shells, bombs, and bullets. But it is doubtful if the day or the night had seen more nerve-trying, courage-testing work, more deliberate and long-drawn bravery than was shown, as a matter of course and as a part of the job, in the digging of that communication trench.

It was done at last, and although it might not be a Class One Exhibition bit of work, it was, as Beefy Wilson remarked, 'a deal better'n none.' And although the trench was already a foot deep in water, Beefy stated no more than bald truth in saying, 'Come to-morrow there's plenty will put up glad wi' their knees bein' below high-water mark for the sake o' havin' their heads below low bullet-mark.'

But, if the trench was finished, the night's work for the Engineers was not. They were moved up into the captured trench, and told that they had to repair it and wire out in front of it before they were done.

They had half an hour's rest before recommencing work, and Beefy Wilson and Jem Duffy hugged the shelter of some tumbled sandbags, lit their pipes and turned the bowls down, and exchanged reminiscences.

'Let's see,' said Beefy. 'Isn't Jigger Adams in your lot?'

'Was,' corrected Jem, 'till an hour ago. 'E's out yon wi' a bullet in 'im--stiff by now.'

Beefy breathed blasphemous regrets. 'Rough on 'is missus an' the kids. Six of 'em, weren't it?'

'Aw,' assented Jem. 'But she'll get suthin' from the Society funds.'

'Not a ha'porth,' said Beefy. 'You'll remem--no, it was just arter you left. The trades unions decided no benefits would be paid out for them as 'listed. It was Ben Shrillett engineered that. 'E was Secretary an' Treasurer an' things o' other societies as well as ours. 'E fought the War right along, an' 'e's still fightin' it. 'E's a anti-militant, 'e ses.'

'Anti-militarist,' Jem corrected. He had taken some pains himself in the old days to get the word itself and some of its meaning right.

'Anti-military-ist then,' said Beefy. 'Any'ow, 'e stuck out agin all sorts o' sol-dierin'. This stoppin' the Society benefits was a trump card too. It blocked a whole crowd from listin' that I know myself would ha' joined. Queered the boss's sons raisin' that Company too. They 'ad Frickers an' the B.S.L. Co. an' the works to draw from. Could ha' raised a couple hundred easy if Ben Shrillett 'adn't got at 'em. You know 'ow 'e talks the fellers round.'

'I know,' agreed Jem, sucking hard at his pipe.

The Sergeant broke in on their talk. 'Now then,' he said briskly. 'Sooner we start, sooner we're done an' off 'ome to our downy couch. 'Ere, Duffy'--and he pointed out the work Duffy was to start.

For a good two hours the Engineers laboured like slaves again. The trench was so badly wrecked that it practically had to be reconstructed. It was dangerous work because it meant moving freely up and down, both where cover was and was not. It was physically heavy work because spade work in wet ground must always be that; and when the spade constantly encounters a debris of broken beams, sandbags, rifles, and other impediments, and the work has to be performed in eye-confusing alternations of black darkness and dazzling flares, it makes the whole thing doubly hard. When you add in the constant whisk of passing bullets and the smack of their striking, the shriek and shattering burst of high-explosive shells, and the drone and whirr of flying splinters, you get labour conditions removed to the utmost limit from ideal, and, to any but the men of the Sappers, well over the edge of the im-possible. The work at any other time would have been gruesome and unnerving, because the gasping and groaning of the wounded hardly ceased from end to end of the captured trench, and in digging out the collapsed sections many dead Germans and some British were found blocking the vigorous thrust of the spades.

Duffy was getting 'fair fed up,' although he still worked on mechanically. He wondered vaguely what Ben Shrillett would have said to any member of the trade union that had worked a night, a day, and a night on end. He wondered, too, how Ben Shrillett would have shaped in the Royal Engineers, and, for all his cracking muscles and the back-breaking weight and unwieldiness of the wet sandbags, he had to grin at the thought of Ben, with his podgy fat fingers and his visible rotundity of waistcoat, sweating and straining there in the wetness and darkness with Death whistling past his ear and crashing in shrapnel bursts about him. The joke was too good to keep to himself, and he passed it to Beefy next time he came near. Beefy saw the jest clearly and guffawed aloud, to the amazement of a clay-daubed infantryman who had had nothing in his mind but thoughts of death and loading and firing his rifle for hours past.

'Don't wonder Ben's agin conscription,' said Beefy; 'they might conscription 'im,' and passed on grinning.

Duffy had never looked at it in that light. He'd been anti-conscription himself, though now--mebbe--he didn't know--he wasn't so sure.

And after the trench was more or less repaired came the last and the most desperate business of all--the 'wiring' out there in the open under the eye of the soaring lights. In ones and twos during the intervals of darkness the men tumbled over the parapet, dragging stakes and coils of wire behind them. They managed to drive short stakes and run trip-wires between them without the enemy suspecting them. When a light flamed, every man dropped flat in the mud and lay still as the dead beside them till the light died. In the brief intervals of darkness they drove the stakes with muffled hammers, and ran the lengths of barbed wire between them. Heart in mouth they worked, one eye on the dimly seen hammer and stake-head, the other on the German trench, watching for the first upward trailing sparks of the flare. Plenty of men were hit of course, because, light or dark, the bullets were kept flying, but there was no pause in the work, not even to help the wounded in. If they were able to crawl they crawled, dropping flat and still while the lights burned, hitching themselves painfully towards the parapet under cover of the darkness. If they could not crawl they lay still, dragging themselves perhaps behind the cover of a dead body or lying quiet in the open till the time would come when helpers would seek them. Their turn came when the low wires were complete. The wounded were brought in cautiously to the trench then, and hoisted over the parapet; the working party was carefully detailed and each man's duty marked out before they crawled again into the open with long stakes and strands of barbed wire. The party lay there minute after minute, through periods of light and darkness, until the officer in charge thought a favourable chance had come and gave the arranged signal. Every man leaped to his feet, the stakes were planted, and quick blow after blow drove them home. Another light soared up and flared out, and every man dropped and held his breath, waiting for the crash of fire that would tell they were discovered. But the flare died out without a sign, and the working party hurriedly renewed their task. This time the darkness held for an unusual length of time, and the stakes were planted, the wires fastened, and cross-pieces of wood with inter-lacings of barbed wire all ready were rolled out and pegged down without another light showing. The word passed down and the men scrambled back into safety.

'Better shoot a light up quick,' said the Engineer officer to the infantry commander. 'They have a working party out now. I heard 'em hammering. That's why they went so long without a light.'

A pistol light was fired and the two stared out into the open ground it lit. 'Thought so,' said the Engineer, pointing. 'New stakes--see? And those fellows lying beside 'em.'

'Get your tools together, sergeant,' he said, as several more lights flamed and a burst of rapid fire rose from the British rifles, 'and collect your party. Our job's done, and I'm not sorry for it.'

It was just breaking daylight when the remains of the Engineers' party emerged from the communication trench and already the guns on both sides were beginning to talk. Beefy Wilson and Jem Duffy between them found Jigger's body and brought it as far as the dressing station. Behind the trenches Beefy's company and Jem's section took different roads, and the two old friends parted with a casual 'S' long' and 'See you again sometime.'

Duffy had two hours' sleep in a sopping wet roofless house, about three miles behind the firing line. Then the section was roused and marched back to their billets in a shell-wrecked village, a good ten miles farther back. They found what was left of the other three sections of the Southland Company there, heard the tale of how the Company had been cut up in advancing with the charging infantry, ate a meal, scraped some of the mud off themselves, and sought their blankets and wet straw beds.

Jem Duffy could not get the thought of Ben Shrillett, labour leader and agitator, out of his mind, and mixed with his thoughts as he went to sleep were that officer's remarks about pressed men. That perhaps accounts for his waking thoughts running on the same groove when his sergeant roused him at black midnight and informed him the section was being turned out--to dig trenches.

'Trenches,' spluttered Sapper Duffy, '. . . us? How is it our turn again?'

'Becos, my son,' said the Sergeant, 'there's nobody else about 'ere to take a turn. Come on! Roll out! Show a leg!'

It was then that Sapper Duffy was finally converted, and renounced for ever and ever his anti-conscription principles.

'Nobody else,' he said slowly, 'an' England fair stiff wi' men. . . . The sooner we get Conscription, the better I'll like it. Conscription solid for every bloomin' able-bodied man an' boy. An' I 'ope Ben Shrillett an' 'is likes is the first to be took. Conscription,' he said with the emphasis of finality as he fumbled in wet straw for a wetter boot, 'out-an'-out, lock, stock, 'n barrel Conscription.'

*   *   *   *   *

That same night Ben Shrillett was presiding at a meeting of the Strike Committee. He had read on the way to the meeting the communique that told briefly of Sapper Duffy and his fellow Engineers' work of the night before, and the descriptive phrase struck him as sounding neat and effective. He worked it now into his speech to the Committee, explaining how and where they and he benefited by this strike, unpopular as it had proved.

'We've vindicated the rights of the workers,' he said. 'We've shown that, war or no war, Labour means to be more than mere wage-slaves. War can't last for ever, and we here, this Committee, proved ourselves by this strike the true leaders and the Champions of Labour, the Guardians of the Rights of Trade Unionism. We, gentlemen, have always been that, and by the strike'--and he concluded with the phrase from the despatch--'we have maintained and consolidated our position.'

The Committee said, 'Hear, hear.' It is a pity they could not have heard what Sapper Duffy was saying as he sat up in his dirty wet straw, listening to the rustle and patter of rain on the barn's leaky roof and tugging on an icy-cold board-stiff boot.

'BUSINESS AS USUAL'

The remains of the Regiment were slowly working their way back out of action. They had been in it for three days--three strenuous nights and days of marching, of fighting, of suffering under heavy shell-fire, of insufficient and broken sleep, of irregular and unpalatable rations, of short commons of water, of nerve-stretching excitement and suspense, all the inevitable discomforts and hardships that in the best organised of armies must be the part of any hard-fought action. The Regiment had suffered cruelly, and their casualties had totalled some sixty per cent. of the strength. And now they were coming back, jaded and worn, filthily grimed and dirty, unshaven, unwashed, footsore, and limping, but still in good heart and able to see a subject for jests and laughter in the sprawling fall of one of their number plunging hastily to shelter from the unexpected rush and crash of a shell, in the sultry stream of remarks from an exasperated private when he discovered a bullet-pierced water-bottle and the loss of his last precious drops of water.

The men were trickling out in slow, thin streams along communication and support trenches, behind broken buildings and walls and barricades, under any cover that screened them from the watchful eyes of the enemy observers perched high in trees and buildings and everywhere they could obtain a good look-out over our lines.

In the minds of the men the thoughts of almost all ran in the same grooves--first and most strongly, because perhaps the oftenest framed in speech, that it was hot--this hot and that hot, hot as so-and-so or such-and-such, according to the annoyance or wit of the speaker; second, and much less clearly defined, a dull satisfaction that they had done their share, and done it well, and that now they were on their way out to all the luxury of plenty of food and sleep, water to drink, water and soap to wash with; third, and increasing in proportion as they got farther from the forward line and the chance of being hit, a great anxiety to reach the rear in safety. The fear of being hit by shell or bullet was a hundred-fold greater than it had been during their part in the action, when the risk was easily a hundred times greater, and more sympathy was expended over one man 'casualtied' coming out than over a score of those killed in the actual fight. It seemed such hard lines, after going through all they had gone through and escaping it scot free, that a man should be caught just when it was all over and he was on the verge of a more or less prolonged spell outside the urgent danger zone.

The engagement was not over yet. It had been raging with varying intensity for almost a week, had resulted in a considerable advance of the British line, and had now resolved itself into a spasmodic series of struggles on the one side to 'make good' the captured ground and steal a few more yards, if possible; on the other, to strengthen the defence against further attacks and to make the captured trenches untenable.

But the struggle now was to the Regiment coming out a matter of almost outside interest, an interest reduced nearly to the level of the newspaper readers' at home, something to read or hear and talk about in the intervals of eating and drinking, of work and amusement and sleep and the ordinary incidents of daily life. Except, of course, that the Regiment always had at the back of this casual interest the more personal one that if affairs went badly their routine existence 'in reserve' might be rudely interrupted and they might be hurried back and flung again into the fight.

But that was unlikely, and meantime there were still stray shells and bullets to be dodged, the rifles and kits were blasphemously heavy, and it was most blasphemously hot. The men were occupied enough in picking their steps in the broken ground, in their plodding, laborious progress, above all in paying heed to the order constantly passing back to 'keep low,' but they were still able to note with a sort of professional interest the damage done to the countryside. A 'small-holding' cottage between the trenches had been shelled and set on fire, and was gutted to the four bare, blackened walls. The ground about it still showed in the little squares and oblongs that had divided the different cultivations, but the difference now was merely of various weeds and rank growths, and the ground was thickly pitted with shell-holes. A length of road was gridironed with deep and laboriously dug trenches, and of the poplars that ran along its edge some were broken off in jagged stumps, some stood with stems as straight and bare as telegraph poles, or half cut through and collapsed like a half-shut knife or an inverted V, with their heads in the dust; others were left with heads snapped off and dangling in grey withered leaves, or with branches glinting white splinters and stripped naked, as in the dead of winter. In an orchard the fruit trees were smashed, uprooted, heaped pell-mell in a tangle of broken branches, bare twisted trunks, fragments of stump a foot or a yard high, here a tree slashed off short, lifted, and flung a dozen yards, and left head down and trunk in air; there a row of currant bushes with a yawning shell-crater in the middle, a ragged remnant of bush at one end and the rest vanished utterly, leaving only a line of torn stems from an inch to a foot long to mark their place.

A farm of some size had been at one time a point in the advanced trenches, and had been converted into a 'keep.' Its late owner would never have recognised it in its new part. Such walls as were left had been buttressed out of sight by sand-bags; trenches twisted about the outbuildings, burrowed under and into them, and wriggled out again through holes in the walls; a market cart, turned upside down, and earthed over to form a bomb-store, occupied a corner of the farmyard; cover for snipers' loopholes had been constructed from ploughshares; a remaining fragment of a grain loft had become an 'observing station'; the farm kitchen a doctor's dressing station; the cow-house a machine-gun place; the cellar, with the stove transplanted from the kitchen, a cooking, eating, and sleeping room. All the roofs had been shelled out of existence. All the walls were notched by shells and peppered thick with bullet marks. A support trench about shoulder deep with a low parapet along its front was so damaged by shell fire that the men for the most part had to move along it bent almost double to keep out of sight and bullet reach. Every here and there--where a shell had lobbed fairly in--there was a huge crater, its sides sealing up the trench with a mass of tumbled earth over which the men scrambled crouching. Behind the trench a stretch of open field was pitted and pock-marked with shell-holes of all sizes from the shallow scoop a yard across to the yawning crater, big and deep enough to bury the whole field-gun that had made the smaller hole. The field looked exactly like those pictures one sees in the magazines of a lunar landscape or the extinct volcanoes of the moon.

The line of men turned at last into a long deep-cut communication trench leading out into a village. The air in the trench was heavy and close and stagnant, and the men toiled wearily up it, sweating and breathing hard. At a branching fork one path was labelled with a neatly printed board 'To Battn. H.Q. and the Mole Heap,' and the other path 'To the Duck Pond'--this last, the name of a trench, being a reminder of the winter and the wet. The officer leading the party turned into the trench for 'The Mole Heap,' walked up it, and emerged into the sunlight of the grass-grown village street, skirted a house, crossed the street by a trench, and passed through a hole chipped out of the brick wall into a house, the men tramping at his heels. The whole village was seamed with a maze of trenches, but these were only for use when the shelling had been particularly heavy. At other times people moved about the place by paths sufficiently well protected by houses and walls against the rifle bullets that had practically never ceased to smack into the village for many months past. These paths wandered behind buildings, across gardens, into and out of houses either by doors or by holes in the wall, over or round piles of rubble or tumbled brick-work, burrowed at times below ground-level on patches exposed to fire, ran frequently through a dozen cottages on end, passage having been effected simply by hacking holes through the connecting brick walls, in one place dived underground down some short stairs and took its way through several cellars by the same simple method of walking through the walls from one cellar to another. The houses were littered with empty and rusty tins, torn and dirty clothing, ash-choked stoves, trampled straw, and broken furniture. The back-yards and gardens were piled with heaps of bricks and tiles, biscuit and jam tins; broken fences and rotted rags were overrun with a rank growth of grass and weeds and flowers, pitted with shell-holes and strewn with graves.

The whole village was wrecked from end to end, was no more than a charnel house, a smashed and battered sepulchre. There was not one building that was whole, not one roof that had more than a few tiles clinging to shattered rafters, hardly a wall that was not cracked and bulged and broken.

In the houses they passed through the men could still find sufficient traces of the former occupants to indicate their class and station. One might have been a labourer's cottage, with a rough deal table, a red-rusted stove-fireplace, an oleograph in flaming crude colours of the 'Virgin and Child' hanging on the plaster wall, the fragments of a rough cradle overturned in a corner, a few coarse china crocks and ornaments and figures chipped and broken and scattered about the mantel, and the bare board floor. Another house had plainly been a home of some refinement. The rooms were large, with lofty ceilings; there were carpets on the floors, although so covered with dirt and dried mud and the dust of fallen plaster that they were hardly discernible as carpets. In one room a large polished table had a broken leg replaced by an up-ended barrel, one big arm-chair had its springs and padding showing through the burst upholstering. Another was minus all its legs, and had the back wrenched off and laid flat with the seat on the floor, evidently to make a bed. There were several good engravings hanging askew on the walls or lying about the floor, all soiled with rain and cut and torn by their splintered glass. The large open-grate fireplace had an artistically carved overmantel sadly chipped and smoke-blackened, a tiled hearth in fragments; the wall-paper in a tasteful design of dark-green and gold was blotched and discoloured, and hung in peeling strips and gigantic 'dog's-ears'; from the poles and rings over the windows the tattered fragments of a lace curtain dangled. There was plenty of evidence that the room had been occupied by others since its lawful tenants had fled. It was strewn with broken or cast-off military equipments, worn-out boots, frayed and mud-caked putties, a burst haversack and pack-valise, a holed water-bottle, broken webbing straps and belts, a bayonet with a snapped blade, a torn grey shirt, and a goatskin coat. The windows had the shutters closed, and were sandbagged up three parts their height, the need for this being evident from the clean, round bullet-holes in the shutters above the sandbags, and the ragged tears and holes in the upper part of the opposite wall. In an upper corner a gaping shell-hole had linen table-cloths five or six fold thick hung over to screen the light from showing through at night. In a corner lay a heap of mouldy straw and a bed-mattress; the table and fireplace were littered with dirty pots and dishes, the floor with empty jam and biscuit tins, opened and unopened bully-beef tins, more being full than empty because the British soldier must be very near starving point before he is driven to eat 'bully.' Over everything lay, like a white winding-sheet, the cover of thick plaster-dust shaken down from the ceiling by the hammer-blows of the shells. The room door opened into a passage. At its end a wide staircase curved up into empty space, the top banisters standing out against the open blue sky. The whole upper storey had been blown off by shell fire and lay in the garden behind the house, a jumble of brickwork, window-frames, tiles, beams, beds and bedroom furniture, linen, and clothes.

These houses were inexpressibly sad and forlorn-looking, with all their privacy and inner homeliness naked and exposed to the passer-by and the staring sunlight. Some were no more than heaps of brick and stone and mortar; but these gave not nearly such a sense of desolation and desertion as those less damaged, as one, for instance, with its front blown completely out, so that one could look into all its rooms, upper and lower and the stairs between, exactly as one looks into those dolls' houses where the front is hinged to swing open.

The village had been on the edge of the fighting zone for months, had been casually shelled each day in normal times, bombarded furiously during every attack or counter-attack. The church, with its spire or tower, had probably been suspected as an artillery observing station by the Germans, and so had drawn a full share of the fire. All that was left of the church itself was one corner of shell-holed walls, and a few roof-beams torn and splintered and stripped of cover. The tower was a broken, jagged, stump--an empty shell, with one side blown almost completely out; the others, or what remained of them, cracked and tottering. The churchyard was a wild chaos of tumbled masonry, broken slates, uprooted and overturned tombstones, jumbled wooden crosses, crucifixes, black wooden cases with fronts of splintered glass, torn wreaths, and crosses of imitation flowers. Amongst the graves yawned huge shell craters; tossed hither and thither amongst the graves and broken monuments and bricks and rubbish were bones and fragments of coffins.

But all the graves were not in the churchyard. The whole village was dotted from end to end with them, some alone in secluded corners, others in rows in the backyards and vegetable gardens. Most of them were marked with crosses, each made of two pieces of packing-case or biscuit-box, with a number, rank, name, and regiment printed in indelible pencil. On some of the graves were bead-work flowers, on others a jam-pot or crock holding a handful of withered sun-dried flower-stalks. Nearly all were huddled in close to house or garden walls, one even in the narrow passage between two houses. There were, in many cases, other and less ugly open spaces and gardens offering a score of paces from these forlorn last resting-places apparently so oddly selected and sadly misplaced; but a second look showed that in each case the grave was dug where some wall or house afforded cover to the burying-party from bullets. In the bright sunlight, half-hidden under or behind heaps of debris, with crosses leaning drunkenly aslant, these graves looked woefully dreary and depressing. But the files of men moving round and between them, or stepping carefully over them, hardly gave them a glance, except where one in passing caught at a leaning cross and thrust it deeper and straighter into the earth. But the men's indifference meant no lack of feeling or respect for the dead. The respect was there, subtle but unmistakable, instanced slightly by the care every man took not to set foot on a grave, by the straightening of that cross, by those withered flowers and dirty wreaths, even as it has been shown scores of times by the men who crawl at risk of their lives into the open between the forward trenches at night to bring in their dead for decent burial.

Outside the shattered village stood the remains of a large factory, and on this the outcoming files of the Regiment converged, and the first arrivals halted to await the rest. What industry the factory had been concerned with it was impossible to tell. It was full of machinery, smashed, bent, twisted, and overturned, all red with rust, mixed up with and in parts covered by stone and brickwork, beams and iron girders, the whole sprinkled over with gleaming fragments of window-glass The outside walls were almost completely knocked flat, tossed helter-skelter outwards or on top of the machinery. The tall chimney--another suspected 'observing post' probably--lay in a heap of broken brickwork with the last yard or two of the base standing up out of the heap, and even in its remaining stump were other ragged shell-holes. A couple of huge boilers had been torn off their brick furnaces by the force of some monster shell and tossed clear yards away. One was poised across the broken outer wall, with one end in the road. The thick rounded plates were bent and dented in like a kicked biscuit-tin, were riddled and pierced through and through as if they had been paper. The whole factory and its machinery must once have represented a value of many thousands of francs. Now it was worth just the value of its site--less the cost of clearing it of debris--and the price of some tons of old iron.

Some of the men wandered about amongst the ruins, examining them curiously, tracing the work of individual shells, speculating on the number of hands the place had once employed, and where those hands were now.

'Man, man,' said a Scottish private, 'sic an awfu' waste. Think o' the siller it must ha' cost.'

''Ow would you like to be a shareholder in the company, Jock?' said his companion. 'Ain't many divvydends due to 'em this Christmas.'

The Scot shook his head sadly. 'This place an' the hale toon laid waste,' he said. 'It's awfu' tae think o' it.'

'An' this is one bloomin' pebble in a whole bloomin' beach,' said the other. 'D'you remember Wipers an' all them other towns? An' that old chap we saw sittin' on the roadside weepin' 'is eyes out 'cos the farm an' the fruit-trees 'e'd spent 'is life fixin' up was blowed to glory b' Jack Johnsons. We 'ave seed some rummy shows 'ere, 'aven't we? Not but what this ain't a pretty fair sample o' wreck,' he continued critically. 'There's plenty 'ud think they'd got their two-pennorth to see this on the screen o' a picture-show at 'ome, Jock.'

'Huh! Picturs!' sniffed Jock. 'Picturs, and the-ayters, and racin', and fitba'. Ah wanner folks hasna better use for their time and money, at sic a time 's this.'

'Aw,' said the other, 'But y' forget, Jock. Out 'ere they 'ave their 'ouses blown up an' their business blown in. A thousan' a day o' the like o' you an' me may be gettin' killed off for six months on end. But at 'ome, Jock--aw!'

He stooped and picked up a lump of white, chalky earth from the roadside, scrawled with it on the huge boiler-end that rested on the broken wall, and left the written words to finish the spoken sentence.

Jock read, and later the remains of the Regiment read as they moved off past the aching desolation of the silent factory, down the shell-torn road, across the war-swept ruins of a whole country-side. A few scowled at the thoughts the words raised, the most grinned and passed rough jests; but to all those men in the thinned ranks, their dead behind them, the scenes of ruin before them, the words bit, and bit deep. They ran:

But it's Bisness As Usual
        --AT HOME.

A HYMN OF HATE

'The troops continue in excellent spirits.'--EXTRACT FROM OFFICIAL DESPATCH.

To appreciate properly, from the Army's point of view, the humour of this story, it must always be remembered that the regiment concerned is an English one--entirely and emphatically English, and indeed almost entirely East End Cockney.

It is true that the British Army on active service has a sense of humour peculiarly its own, and respectable civilians have been known, when jests were retailed with the greatest gusto by soldier raconteurs, to shudder and fail utterly to understand that there could be any humour in a tale so mixed up with the grim and ghastly business of killing and being killed.

A biggish battle had died out about a week before in the series of spasmodic struggles of diminishing fury that have characterised most of the battles on the Western Front, when the Tower Bridge Foot found themselves in occupation of a portion of the forward line which was only separated from the German trench by a distance varying from forty to one hundred yards. Such close proximity usually results in an interchange of compliments between the two sides, either by speech, or by medium of a board with messages written on it--the board being reserved usually for the strokes of wit most likely to sting, and therefore best worth conveying to the greatest possible number of the enemy.

The 'Towers' were hardly installed in their new position when a voice came from the German parapet, 'Hello, Tower Bridge Foot! Pleased to meet you again.'

The Englishmen were too accustomed to it to be surprised by this uncannily prompt recognition by the enemy of a newly relieving regiment of which they had not seen so much as a cap top.

'Hullo, Boshy,' retorted one of the Towers. 'You're makin' a mistake this time. We ain't the Tower Bridges. We're the Kamchatka 'Ighlanders.'

'An' you're a liar if you says you're pleased to meet us again,' put in another. 'If you've met us afore I lay you was too dash sorry for it to want to meet us again.'

'Oh, we know who you are all right,' replied the voice. 'And we know you've just relieved the Fifth Blankshires; and what's more, we know who's going to relieve you, and when.'

''E knows a bloomin' heap,' said a Tower Bridge private disgustedly; 'an' wot's more, I believe 'e does know it.' Then, raising his voice, he asked, 'Do you know when we're comin' to take some more of them trenches o' yours?'

This was felt by the listening Towers to be a master-stroke, remembering that the British had taken and held several trenches a week before, but the reply rather took the wind out of their sails.

'You can't take any more,' said the voice. 'You haven't shells enough for another attack. You had to stop the last one because your guns were running short.'

'Any'ow,' replied an English corporal who had been handing round half a dozen grenades, 'we ain't anyways short o' bombs. 'Ave a few to be goin' on with,' and he and his party let fly. They listened with satisfaction to the bursts, and through their trench periscopes watched the smoke and dust clouds billowing from the trench opposite.

'An' this,' remarked a Tower private, 'is about our cue to exit, the stage bein' required for a scene-shift by some Bosh bombs,' and he disappeared, crawling into a dug-out. During the next ten minutes a couple of dozen bombs came over and burst in and about the British trench and scored three casualties, 'slightly wounded.'

'Hi there! Where's that Soho barber's assistant that thinks 'e can talk Henglish?' demanded the Towers' spokesman cheerfully.

That annoyed the English-speaking German, as of course incidentally it was meant to do.

'I'm here, Private Petticoat Lane,' retorted the voice, 'and if I couldn't speak better English than you I'd be shaming Soho.'

'You're doing that anyway, you bloomin' renegade dog-stealer,' called back the private. 'Wy didn't you pay your landlady in Lunnon for the lodgin's you owed when you run away?'

'Schweinhund!' said the voice angrily, and a bullet slapped into the parapet in front of the taunting private.

'Corp'ril,' said that artist in invective softly, 'if you'll go down the trench a bit or up top o' that old barn behind I'll get this bloomin' Soho waiter mad enough to keep on shootin' at me, an' you'll p'raps get a chance to snipe 'im.'

The corporal sought an officer's permission and later a precarious perch on the broken roof of the barn, while Private Robinson extended himself in the manufacture of annoying remarks.

'That last 'un was a fair draw, Smithy,' he exulted to a fellow private. 'I'll bet 'e shot the moon, did a bolt for it, when 'e mobilised.'

'Like enough,' agreed Smithy. 'Go on, ol' man. Give 'im some more jaw.'

'I s'pose you left without payin' your washin' bill either, didn't you, sowerkrowt,' demanded Private Robinson. There was no reply from the opposition.

'I expeck you ler' a lot o' little unpaid bills, didn't you?--if you was able to find anyone to give you tick.'

'I'll pay them--when we take London,' said the voice.

'That don't give your pore ol' landlady much 'ope,' said Robinson. 'Take Lunnon! Blimy, you're more like to take root in them trenches o' yours--unless we comes over again an' chases you out.'

Again there was no reply. Private Robinson shook his head. "E's as 'ard to draw as the pay that's owin' to me,' he said. 'You 'ave a go, Smithy.'

Smithy, a believer in the retort direct and no trafficker in the finer shades of sarcasm, cleared his throat and lifted up his voice. "Ere, why don't you speak when you're spoke to, you lop-eared lager-beer barrel, you. Take your fice out o' that 'orse-flesh cat's-meat sossidge an' speak up, you baby-butcherin' hen-roost robber.'

'That ain't no good, Smithy,' Private Robinson pointed out. 'Y'see, callin' 'im 'ard names only makes 'im think 'e's got you angry like--that 'e's drawed you.'

(Another voice called something in German.)

'Just tell them other monkeys to stop their chatter, Soho,' he called out, 'an' get back in their cage. If they want to talk to gen'l'men they must talk English.'

'I like your d--d impertinence,' said the voice scornfully. 'We'll make you learn German, though, when we've taken England.'

'Oh, it's Englan' you're takin' now,' said Private Robinson. 'But all you'll ever take of Englan' will be same as you took before--a tuppenny tip if you serves the soup up nice, or a penny tip if you gives an Englishman a proper clean shave.'

The rifle opposite banged again and the bullet slapped into the top of the parapet. 'That drawed 'im again,' chuckled Private Robinson, 'but I wonder why the corp'ril didn't get a whack at 'im.'

He pulled away a small sandbag that blocked a loophole, and, holding his rifle by the butt at arm-length, poked the muzzle out slowly. A moment later two reports rang out--one from in front and one behind.

'I got 'im,' said the corporal three minutes later. 'One bloke was looking with a periscope and I saw a little cap an' one eye come over the parapet. By the way 'is 'ands jerked up an' 'is 'ead jerked back when I fired, I fancy 'e copped it right enough.'

Private Robinson got to work with a piece of chalk on a board and hoisted over the parapet a notice, 'R.I.P. 1 Boshe, late lamented Soho garcon.'

'Pity I dunno the German for "late lamented," but they've always plenty that knows English enough to unnerstand,' he commented.

He spent the next ten minutes ragging the Germans, directing his most brilliant efforts of sarcasm against made-in-Germany English-speakers generally and Soho waiters in particular; and he took the fact there was no reply from the voice as highly satisfactory evidence that it had been the 'Soho waiter' who had 'copped it.'

'Exit the waiter--curtain, an' soft music!' remarked a private known as 'Enery Irving throughout the battalion, and whistled a stave of 'We shall meet, but we shall miss him.'

'Come on, 'Enery, give us 'is dyin' speech,' some one urged, and 'Enery proceeded to recite an impromptu 'Dyin' Speech of the Dachshund-stealer,' as he called it, in the most approved fashion of the East End drama, with all the accompaniments of rolling eyes, breast-clutchings, and gasping pauses.

'Now then, where's the orchestra?' he demanded when the applause had subsided, and the orchestra, one mouth-organ strong, promptly struck up a lilting music-hall ditty. From that he slid into 'My Little Grey Home,' with a very liberal measure of time to the long-drawn notes especially. The song was caught up and ran down the trench in full chorus. When it finished the orchestra was just on the point of starting another tune, when 'Enery held up his hand.

'"'E goes on Sunday to the church, an' sits among the choir,"' he quoted solemnly and added, 'Voices 'eard, off.'

Two or three men were singing in the German trench, and as they sang the rest joined in and 'Deutschland ueber Alles' rolled forth in full strength and harmony.

'Bray-vo! An' not arf bad neither,' said Private Robinson approvingly. 'Though I dunno wot it's all abart. Now s'pose we gives 'em another.'

They did, and the Germans responded with 'The Watch on the Rhine.' This time Private Robinson and the rest of the Towers recognised the song and capped it in great glee with 'Winding up the Watch on the Rhine,' a parody which does not go out of its way to spare German feelings.

'An' 'ow d'you like that, ol' sossidge scoffers?' demanded Private Robinson loudly.

'You vait,' bellowed a guttural voice. 'Us vind you op--quick!'

'Vind op--squeak, an' squeakin',' retorted Private Robinson.

The German reply was drowned in a burst of new song which ran like wild-fire the length of the German trench. A note of fierce passion rang in the voices, and the Towers sat listening in silence.

'Dunno wot it is,' said one. 'But it sounds like they was sayin' something nasty, an' meanin' it all.'

But one word, shouted fiercely and lustily, caught Private Robinson's ear.

''Ark!' he said in eager anticipation. 'I do believe it's--s-sh! There!' triumphantly, as again the word rang out--the one word at the end of the verse . . . 'England.'

'It's *it*. It's the "'Ymn of 'Ate"!'

The word flew down the British trench--'It's the 'Ymn! They're singin' the "'Ymn of 'Ate,"' and every man sat drinking the air in eagerly. This was luck, pure gorgeous luck. Hadn't the Towers, like many another regiment, heard about the famous 'Hymn of Hate,' and read it in the papers, and had it declaimed with a fine frenzy by Private 'Enery Irving? Hadn't they, like plenty other regiments, longed to hear the tune, but longed in vain, never having found one who knew it? And here it was being sung to them in full chorus by the Germans themselves. Oh, this *was* luck.

The mouth-organist was sitting with his mouth open and his head turned to listen, as if afraid to miss a single note.

''Ave you got it, Snapper?' whispered Private Robinson anxiously at the end. 'Will you be able to remember it?'

Snapper, with his eyes fixed on vacancy, began to play the air over softly, when from further down the trench came a murmur of applause, that rose to a storm of hand-clappings and shouts of 'Bravo!' and 'Encore--'core--'core!'

The mouth-organist played on unheedingly and Private Robinson sat following him with attentive ear.

'I'm not sure of that bit just there,' said the player, and tried it over with slight variations. 'P'raps I'll remember it better after a day or two. I'm like that wi' some toons.'

'We might kid 'em to sing it again,' said Robinson hopefully, as another loud cry of 'Encore!' rang from the trench.

'Was you know vat we haf sing?' asked a German voice in tones of some wonderment.

'It's a great song, Dutchie,' replied Private Robinson. 'Fine song--goot--bong! Sing it again to us.'

'You haf not understand,' said the German angrily, and then suddenly from a little further along the German trench a clear tenor rose, singing the Hymn in English. The Towers subsided into rapt silence, hugging themselves over their stupendous luck. When the singer came to the end of the verse he paused an instant, and a roar leaped from the German trench . . . 'England!' It died away and the singer took up the solo. Quicker and quicker he sang, the song swirling upward in a rising note of passion. It checked and hung an instant on the last line, as a curling wave hangs poised; and even as the falling wave breaks thundering and rushing, so the song broke in a crash of sweeping sound along the line of the German trench on that one word--'England!'

Before the last sound of it had passed, the singer had plunged into the next verse, his voice soaring and shaking with an intensity of feeling. The whole effect was inspiring, wonderful, dramatic. One felt that it was emblematic, the heart and soul of the German people poured out in music and words. And the scorn, the bitter anger, hatred, and malice that vibrated again in that chorused last word might well have brought fear and trembling to the heart of an enemy. But the enemy immediately concerned, to wit His Majesty's Regiment of Tower Bridge Foot, were most obviously not impressed with fear and trembling. Impressed they certainly were. Their applause rose in a gale of clappings and cries and shouts. They were impressed, and Private 'Enery Irving, clapping his hands sore and stamping his feet in the trench-bottom, voiced the impression exactly. 'It beats Saturday night in the gallery o' the old Brit.,' he said enthusiastically. 'That bloke--blimy--'e ought to be doin' the star part at Drury Lane'; and he wiped his hot hands on his trousers and fell again to beating them together, palms and fingers curved cunningly, to obtain a maximum of noise from the effort. An officer passed hurriedly along the trench. 'If there's any firing, every man to fire over the parapet and only straight to his own front,' he said, and almost at the moment there came a loud 'bang' from out in front, followed quickly by 'bang-bang-bang' in a running series of reports.

The shouting had cut off instantly on the first bang, some rifles squibbed off at intervals for a few seconds and increased suddenly to a sputtering roar. With the exception of one platoon near their centre the Towers replied rapidly to the fire, the maxims joined in, and a minute later, with a whoop and a crash the shells from a British battery passed over the trench and burst along the line of the German parapet. After that the fire died away gradually, and about ten minutes later a figure scrambled hastily over the parapet and dropped into safety, his boots squirting water, his wet shirt-tails flapping about his bare wet and muddy legs. He was the 'bomb officer' who had taken advantage of the 'Hymn of Hate' diversion to go crawling up a little ditch that crossed the neutral ground until he was near enough to fling into the German trench the bombs he carried, and, as he put it later in reporting to the O.C., 'give 'em something to hate about.'

And each evening after that, for as long as they were in the trenches, the men of the Tower Bridge Foot made a particular point of singing the 'Hymn of Hate,' and the wild yell of 'England' that came at the end of each verse might almost have pleased any enemy of England's instead of aggravating them intensely, as it invariably did the Germans opposite, to the extent of many wasted rounds.

'It's been a great do, Snapper,' said Private 'Enery Irving some days after, as the battalion tramped along the road towards 'reserve billets.' 'An' I 'aven't enjoyed myself so much for months. Didn't it rag 'em beautiful, an' won't we fair stagger the 'ouse at the next sing-sing o' the brigade?'

Snapper chuckled and breathed contentedly into his beloved mouth-organ, and first 'Enery and then the marching men took up the words:

'Ite of the 'eart, an' 'ite of the 'and, 'Ite by water, an' 'ite by land, 'Oo do we 'ite to beat the band?

(deficient memories, it will be noticed, being compensated by effective inventions in odd lines).

The answering roar of 'England' startled almost to shying point the horse of a brigadier trotting up to the tail of the column.

'What on earth are those fellows singing?' he asked one of his officers while soothing his mount.

'I'm not sure, sir,' said the officer, 'but I believe--by the words of it--yes, it's the Germans' "Hymn of Hate."'

A French staff officer riding with the brigadier stared in astonishment, first at the marching men, and then at the brigadier, who was rocking with laughter in his saddle.

'Where on earth did they get the tune? I've never heard it before,' said the brigadier, and tried to hum it. The staff officer told him something of the tale as he had heard it, and the Frenchman's amazement and the brigadier's laughter grew as the tale was told.

We 'ave one foe, an' one alone--England!

bellowed the Towers, and out of the pause that came so effectively before the last word of the verse rose a triumphant squeal from the mouth-organ, and the appealing voice of Private 'Enery Irving--'Naw then, put a bit of 'ate into it.' But even that artist of the emotions had to admit his critical sense of the dramatic fully satisfied by the tone of vociferous wrath and hatred flung into the Towers' answering roar of '. . . . *England!*'

'What an extraordinary people!' said the French staff officer, eyeing the brigadier shaking with laughter on his prancing charger. And he could only heave his shoulders up in an ear-embracing shrug of non-comprehension when the laughing brigadier tried to explain to him (as I explained to you in the beginning):

'And the best bit of the whole joke is that this particular regiment is English to the backbone.'

THE COST

'The cost in casualties cannot be considered heavy in view of the success gained.'--EXTRACT FROM OFFICIAL DESPATCH.

Outside there were blazing sunshine and heat, a haze of smoke and dust, a nostril-stinging reek of cordite and explosive, and a never-ceasing tumult of noises. Inside was gloom, but a closer, heavier heat, a drug-shop smell, and all the noises of outside, little subdued, and mingled with other lesser but closer sounds. Outside a bitterly fought trench battle was raging; here, inside, the wreckage of battle was being swiftly but skilfully sorted out, classified, bound up, and despatched again into the outer world. For this was one of the field dressing stations scattered behind the fringe of the fighting line, and through one or other of these were passing the casualties as quickly as they could be collected and brought back. The station had been a field labourer's cottage, and had been roughly adapted to its present use. The interior was in semi-darkness, because the windows were completely blocked up with sandbags. The door, which faced towards the enemy's lines, was also sandbagged up, and a new door had been made by knocking out an opening through the mud-brick wall. There were two rooms connected by a door, enlarged again by the tearing down of the lath-and-plaster partition. The only light in the inner room filtered through the broken and displaced tiles of the roof. On the floor, laid out in rows so close packed that there was barely room for an orderly to move, were queer shapeless bundles that at first glance could hardly be recognised as men. They lay huddled on blankets or on the bare floor in dim shadowy lines that were splashed along their length with irregularly placed gleaming white patches. They were puzzling, these patches, shining like snow left in the hollows of a mountain seen far off and in the dusk. A closer look revealed them as the bandages of the first field dressing that every man carries stitched in his uniform against the day he or the stretcher-bearers may rip open the packet to use it. A few of the men moved restlessly, but most lay very still. A few talked, and one or two even laughed; and another moaned slowly and at even unbroken intervals. Two or three lighted cigarettes pin-pricked the gloom in specks of orange light that rose and fell, glowing and sparkling and lighting a faint outline of nose and lip and cheeks, sinking again to dull red. A voice called, feebly at first, and then, as no one answered, more strongly and insistently, for water. When at last it was brought, every other man there demanded or pleaded for a drink.

In the other room a clean-edged circle of light blazed in the centre from an acetylene lamp, leaving the walls and corners in a shadow deep by contrast to blackness. Half the length of a rough deal table jutted out of the darkness into the circle of light, and beneath it its black shadow lay solid half-way across the light ring on the floor.

And into this light passed a constant procession of wounded, some halting for no more than the brief seconds necessary for a glance at the placing of a bandage and an injection of an anti-tetanus serum, some waiting for long pain-laden minutes while a bandage was stripped off, an examination made, in certain cases a rapid play made with cruel-looking scissors and knives. Sometimes a man would walk to the table and stoop a bandaged head or thrust a bandaged hand or arm into the light. Or a stretcher would appear from the darkness and be laid under the light, while the doctors' hands busied themselves about the khaki form that lay there. Some of the wounds were slight, some were awful and unpleasant beyond telling. The doctors worked in a high pressure of haste, but the procession never halted for an instant; one patient was hardly clear of the light-circle before another appeared in it. There were two doctors there--one a young man with a lieutenant's stars on his sleeve; the other, apparently a man of about thirty, in bare arms with rolled-up shirt-sleeves. His jacket, hooked on the back of a broken chair, bore the badges of a captain's rank. The faces of both as they caught the light were pale and glistening with sweat. The hands of both as they flitted and darted about bandages or torn flesh were swift moving, but steady and unshaking as steel pieces of machinery. Words that passed between the two were brief to curtness, technical to the last syllable. About them the dust motes danced in the light, the air hung heavy and stagnant, smelling of chemicals, the thick sickly scent of blood, the sharper reek of sweat. And everything about them, the roof over their heads, the walls around, the table under their hands, the floor beneath their feet, shook and trembled and quivered without cessation. And also without pause the uproar of battle bellowed and shrieked and pounded in their ears. Shells were streaming overhead, the closer ones with a rush and a whoop, the higher and heavier ones with long whistling sighs and screams. Shells exploding near them crashed thunderously and set the whole building rocking more violently than ever. The rifle and machine-gun fire never ceased, but rose and fell, sinking at times to a rapid spluttering crackle, rising again to a booming drum-like roll. The banging reports of bombs and grenades punctuated sharply the running roar of gun and rifle fire.

Through all the whirlwind of noise the doctors worked steadily. Unheeding the noise, the dust, the heat, the trembling of the crazy building, they worked from dawn to noon, and from noon on again to dusk, only pausing for a few minutes at mid-day to swallow beef-tea and a biscuit, and in the afternoon to drink tepid tea. Early in the afternoon a light shell struck a corner of the roof, making a clean hole on entry and blowing out the other side in a clattering gust of flame and smoke, broken tiles and splintering wood. The room filled with choking smoke and dust and bitter blinding fumes, and a shower of dirt and fragments rained down on the floor and table, on the doctors, and on the men lying round the walls. At the first crash and clatter some of the wounded cried out sharply, but one amongst them chided the others, asking had they never heard a Fizz-Bang before, and what would the Doctor be thinking of them squealing there like a lot of schoolgirls at a mouse in the room? But later in the day there was a worse outcry and a worse reason for it. The second room was being emptied, the wounded being carried out to the ambulances that awaited them close by outside. There came suddenly out of the surrounding din of battle four quick car-filling rushes of sound--sh-sh-sh-shoosh--ba-ba-ba-bang! The shells had passed over no more than clear of the cottage, and burst in the air just beyond, and for an instant the stretcher-bearers halted hesitatingly and the wounded shrank on their stretchers. But next instant the work was resumed, and was in full swing when a minute later there came again the four wind-rushes, followed this time by four shattering crashes, an appalling clatter of whirling tiles and brick-work. The cottage disappeared in swirling clouds of smoke and brick-dust, and out of the turmoil came shrieks and cries and groans. When the dust had cleared it showed one end of the cottage completely wrecked, the roof gone, the walls gaping in ragged rents, the end wall collapsed in jumbled ruins. Inside the room was no more than a shambles. There were twenty odd men in it when the shells struck. Seven were carried out alive, and four of these died in the moving. In the other room, where the two doctors worked, no damage was done beyond the breakdown of a portion of the partition wall, and there was only one further casualty--a man who was actually having a slight hand-wound examined at the moment. He was killed instantly by a shell fragment which whizzed through the door-way. The two doctors, after a first hasty examination of the new casualties, held a hurried consultation. The obvious thing to do was to move, but the question was, Where to? One place after another was suggested, only for the suggestion to be dismissed for some good and adequate reason. In the middle of the discussion a fresh torrent of casualties began to pour in. Some plainly required immediate at-tention, and the doctors fell to work again. By the time the rush was cleared the question of changing position had been forgotten, or, at any rate, was dropped. The wounded continued to arrive, and the doctors continued to work.

By now, late afternoon, the fortunes of the fight were plainly turning in favour of the British. It was extraordinary the difference it made in the whole atmosphere--to the doctors, the orderlies, the stretcher-bearers, and even--or, rather, most of all--to the wounded who were coming in. In the morning the British attack had been stubbornly withstood, and thousands of men had fallen in the first rushes to gain a footing in the trenches opposite. The wounded who were first brought in were the men who had fallen in these rushes, in the forward trench, in the com-munication trenches on their way up from the support trench, and from the shell fire on the support trenches. Because they themselves had made no advance, or had seen no advance made, they believed the attack was a failure, that thousands of men had fallen and no ground had been gained. The stretcher-bearers who brought them in had a similar tale to tell, and everyone looked glum and pulled a long face. About noon, although the advance on that particular portion was still hung up, a report ran that success had been attained elsewhere along the line. In the early afternoon the guns behind burst out in a fresh paroxysm of fury, and the shells poured streaming overhead and drenched the enemy trenches ahead with a new and greater deluge of fire. The rifle fire and the bursting reports of bombs swelled suddenly to the fullest note yet attained. All these things were hardly noted, or at most were heeded with a half-attention, back in the dressing station, but it was not long before the fruits of the renewed activity began to filter and then to flood back to the doctor's hands. But now a new and more encouraging tale came with them. We were winning . . . we were advancing . . . we were into their trenches all along the line. The casualties bore their wounds to the station with absolute cheerfulness. This one had 'got it' in the second line of trenches; that one had seen the attack launched on the third trench; another had heard we had taken the third in our stride and were pushing on hard. The regiment had had a hammering, but they were going good; the battalion had lost the O.C. and a heap of officers, but they were 'in wi' the bayonet' at last. So the story ran for a full two hours. It was borne back by men with limbs and bodies hacked and broken and battered, but with lips smiling and babbling words of triumph. There were some who would never walk, would never stand upright again, who had nothing before them but the grim life of a helpless cripple. There were others who could hardly hope to see the morrow's sun rise, and others again grey-faced with pain and with white-knuckled hands clenched to the stretcher-edges. But all, slightly wounded, or 'serious,' or 'danger-ous,' seemed to have forgotten their own bitter lot, to have no thought but to bear back the good word that 'we're winning.'

Late in the afternoon the weary doctors sensed a slackening in the flowing tide of casualties. They were still coming in, being attended to and passed out in a steady stream, but somehow there seemed less rush, less urgency, less haste on the part of the bearers to be back for a fresh load. And--ominous sign--there were many more of the bearers themselves coming back as casualties. The reason for these things took little finding. The fighting line was now well advanced, and every yard of ad-vance meant additional time and risk in the bearing back of the wounded.

One of the regimental stretcher-bearers put the facts bluntly and briefly to the doctors: 'The open ground an' the communication trenches is fair hummin' wi' shells an' bullets. We're just about losin' two bearers for every one casualty we bring out. Now we're leavin' 'em lie there snug as we can till dark.'

A chaplain came in and asked permission to stay there. 'One of my regiments has gone up, he said, 'and they'll bring the casualties in here. I won't get in your way, and I may be able to help a little. Here is one of my men now.'

A stretcher was carried in and laid with its burden under the doctor's hands. The man was covered with wounds from head to foot. He lay still while the doctors cut the clothing off him and adjusted bandages, but just before they gave him morphia he spoke. 'Don't let me die, doctor,' he said; 'for Christ's sake, don't let me die. Don't say I'm going to die.' His eye met the chaplain's, and the grey head stooped near to the young one. 'I'm the only one left, padre,' he said. 'My old mother. . . . Don't let me die, padre. You know how--it is, back home. Don't--let me--die--too.'

But the lad was past saving. He died there on the table under their hands.

'God help his mother!' said the chaplain softly. 'It was her the boy was thinking of--not himself. His father was killed yesterday--old Jim Doherty, twenty-three years' service; batman to the O.C.; would come out again with young Jim and Walt. Been with the Regiment all his life; and the Regiment has taken him and his two boys, and left the mother to her old age without husband or chick or child.'

The two doctors were lighting cigarettes and inhaling the smoke deeply, with the enjoyment that comes after hours without tobacco.

Another man was borne in. He was grimed with dust and dirt, and smeared with blood. The sweats of agony beaded his forehead, but he grinned a twisted grin at the doctors and chaplain. 'An' 'ere we are again, as the song says,' he said, as the stretcher was laid down. 'This makes the third time wounded in this war--twice 'ome an' out again. But this is like to be the last trip I'm thinkin'. Wot about it, sir? Will I be losin' 'em both?' And he looked down at his smashed legs. 'Ah, I thought so,' he went on. 'I'm a market gardener, but I dunno 'ow I'm goin' to market-garden without legs. Four kids too, the eldest six years, an' an ailin' wife. But she'll 'ave me, or wot's left o' me; an' that's more'n a many'll 'ave.'

'That'll be all right, my lad,' said the chaplain. 'You'll have a pension. The country will look after you.'

'Ah, padre--I didn't see you, sir. The country? Arst my brother Joe about the country. Wounded in South Africa 'e was, an' never done a day's work since. An' the pension 'as been barely enough to starve on decently. It'll be the same again arter all this is over I don't doubt. Any'ow that's 'ow we all feels about it. No, sir, I don't feel no great pain to speak of. Sort of numb-like below there just.'

He went on talking quite rationally and composedly until he was taken away.

After that there was another pause, and the ambulances, for the first time that day, were able to get the station cleared before a fresh lot came in. The dusk was closing in, but there was still no abatement of the sounds of battle.

'There must be crowds of men lying out in front there wanting attention,' said the captain, reaching for his coat and putting it on quietly. 'You might stay here, Dewar, and I'll have a look out and see if there's a chance of getting forward to give a hand.'

The other doctor offered to go if the other would wait, but his offer was quietly put aside. 'I'll get back in an hour or two,' the captain said, and went off. Dewar and the chaplain stood in the door and watched him go. A couple of heavy shells crashed down on the parapet of the communication trench he was moving towards, and for a minute his figure was hidden by the swirling black smoke and yellow dust. But they saw him a moment later as he reached the trench, turned and waved a hand to them, and disappeared.

'His name's Macgillivray,' said the doctor, in answer to a question from the chaplain. 'One of the finest fellows I've ever met, and one of the cleverest surgeons in Great Britain. He is recognised as one of the best already, and he's only begin-ning. Did you notice him at work? The most perfect hands, and an eye as quick and keen as an eagle's. He misses nothing--sees little things in a flash where twenty men might pass them. He's a wonder.'

And Macgillivray was moving slowly along the communication trench that led to the forward fire trench. It was a dangerous passage, because the enemy's guns had the position and range exactly and were keeping a constant fire on the trench, knowing the probability of the supports using it. In fact the supports moving up had actually abandoned the use of the approach trenches and were hurrying across the open for the most part. Macgillivray, reluctant at first to abandon the cover of the trench, was driven at last to doing so by a fact forced upon him at every step that the place was a regular shell-trap. Sections of it were blown to shapeless ruins, and pits and mounds of earth and the deep shell-craters gaped in it and to either side for all its length. Even where the high-explosive shells had not fallen the shrapnel had swept and the clouds of flies that swarmed at every step told of the blood-soaked ground, even where the torn fragments of limbs and bodies had not been left, as they were in many places.

So Macgillivray left the trench and scurried across the open with bullets hissing and buzzing about his ears and shells roaring overhead. He reached the forward fire trench at last and halted there to recover his breath. The battered trench was filled with the men who had been moved up in support, and there were many wounded amongst them. He busied himself for half an hour amongst them, and then prepared to move on across the open to what had been the enemy's front-line trench. It was dusk now and shadowy figures could be seen coming back towards the British lines. At one point, a dip in the ground and an old ditch gave some cover from the flying bullets. Towards this point along what had been the face and was now the back of the enemy front trench, and then in along the line of the hollow, a constant procession of wounded moved slowly. It was easy to distinguish them, and even to pick out in most cases where they were wounded, because in the dusk the bandages of the first field dressing showed up startlingly white and clear on the shadowy forms against the shadowy background. Some, with the white patches on heads, arms, hands, and upper bodies, were walking; others, with the white on feet and legs, limped and hobbled painfully, leaning on the parapet or using their rifles crutch-wise; and others lay on the stretchers that moved with desperate slowness towards safety. The line appeared unending; the dim figures could be seen trickling along the parapets as far as the eye could distinguish them; the white dots of the bandages were visible moving as far along the parapet as the sight could could reach.

Macgillivray moved out from the broken trench and hurried across the open. There were not more than fifty yards to cross, but in that narrow space the bodies lay huddled singly and heaped in little clumps. They reminded one exactly of the loafers who sprawl asleep and sunning themselves in the Park on a Sunday afternoon. Only the dead lay in that narrow strip; the living had been moved or had moved themselves long since. Macgillivray pushed on into the trench, along it to a communication trench, and up and down one alley after another, until he reached the most advanced trench which the British held. Here a pandemonium of fighting was still in progress, but to this Macgillivray after the first couple of minutes paid no heed. A private with a bullet through his throat staggered back from his loophole and collapsed in the doctor's arms and after that Macgillivray had his hands too full with casualties to concern himself with the fighting. Several dug-outs had been filled with wounded, and the doctor crawled about amongst these and along the trench, applying dressings and bandages as fast as he could work, seeing the men placed on stretchers or sent back as quickly as possible towards the rear. He stayed there until a message reached him by one of the stretcher-bearers who had been back to the dressing station that he was badly needed there, and that Mr. Dewar hoped he would get back soon to help them.

Certainly the dressing station was having a busy time. The darkness had made it possible to get back hundreds of casualties from places whence they dare not be moved by day. They were pouring into the station through the doctors' hands-- three of them were hard at work there by this time--and out again to the ambu- lances as rapidly as they could be handled. Despite the open, shell-wrecked end and the broken roof, the cottage was stiflingly close and sultry, the heavy scent of blood hung sickeningly in the stagnant air, and the whole place swarmed with pestering flies. There was no time to do much for the patients. All had been more or less efficiently bandaged by the regimental stretcher-bearers who picked them up. The doctors did little more than examine the bandagings, loosening these and tightening those, making injections to ward off tetanus, performing an operation or an amputation now and again in urgent cases, sorting out occasionally a hopeless casualty where a wound was plainly mortal, and setting him aside to leave room in the ambulances for those the hospitals below might yet save.

One of these mortal cases was a young lieutenant. He knew himself that there was little or no hope for him, but he smoked a cigarette and spoke with composure, or simulated composure, to the doctor and the chaplain.

'Hello, padre,' he said, 'looks like a wash-out for me this time. You'll have to break it to the pater, you know. Afraid he'll take it rather hard too. Rough luck, isn't it, doc.? But then . . .' His face twitched with pain, but he covered the break in his voice by blowing a long cloud of smoke. '. . . After all, it's all in the game, y' know.' 'All in the game,' the chaplain said when he had gone; 'a cruel game, but gallantly played out. And he's the fourth son to go in this war--and the last male of his line except his father, the old earl. A family that has made its mark on a good few history pages--and this is the end of it. You think it's quite hopeless for him, doctor?'

The doctor looked up in surprise from the fresh slightly wounded case he was overhauling. 'Hopeless? Why, it's not even---- Oh! him? Yes, I'm afraid so. . . . I wish Macgillivray would come back,' he went on irritably. 'He's worth the three of us here put together. Where we have to fiddle and probe and peer he would just look--just half-shut those hawk eyes of his and look, and he'd know exactly what to do and what not to do. . . . That'll do, sergeant; take him off. . . . Where's that bottle of mine? What's this? Hand? Bandage not hurting you? All right. Pass him over there for the anti-tetanus. Now, then! . . .'

A burly private, with the flesh of his thigh showing clear white where the grimy khaki had been cut clear and hung flapping, limped in and pushed forward a neatly bandaged limb for inspection. 'A doctor did that up in the trenches,' he remarked. 'Said to tell you 'e did it an' it was all right, an' I only needed the anti-tempus an' a ticket for 'ome.'

'That's Macgillivray, I'll bet,' said young Dewar. 'Where was this?'

'Fourth German trench, sir,' said the man cheerfully. 'You know we got four? Four trenches took! We're winnin' this time orright. Fairly got 'em goin', I b'lieve. It'll be Glorious Vict'ry in the 'eadlines to-morrow.'

'Things like this, you know, must be,' quoted the chaplain softly, as another badly wounded man was brought in. 'I wonder what the victory is costing us?'

'Never mind. It's costing t'other side more, sir,' said the casualty grimly, and then shut lips and teeth tight on the agony that followed.

'I wish Macgillivray would come,' said Dewar when that was finished. 'He could have done it so much better. It's just the sort of case he's at his best on-- and his best is something the medical journals write columns about. I wish he'd come.'

And then, soon after, he did come--came on a stretcher with a bandage about his head and over his eyes. 'Macgillivray!' cried the young doctor, and stood a moment staring, with his jaw dropped.

'Yes,' said Macgillivray with lips tight drawn. 'It's me. That's Dewar, isn't it? No need to undo the bandage, Dewar. It's my eyes--both gone--a bullet through them both. And I'll never hold a scalpel again. You can give me some morphia, Dewar--and send me on to the ambulance out of the way. I'm no good here now-- or anywhere else, now or ever. I won't die, I know, but----'

They gave him the morphia, and before he slid off into unconsciousness he spoke a last word to the chaplain: 'You were right, padre. You remember . . . it's the women pay the hardest. . . . I'm thinking . . . of . . . my wife.'

The chaplain's thoughts went back to the wife and mother of the Dohertys, to the legless market-gardener and his ailing wife, to the boy lieutenant who was the last of his line, and a score more he knew, and his eyes followed as the stretcher bore out the hulk that had been a man who had done much to relieve pain and might have done so much more.

The voice of another new-arriving casualty broke his thoughts. 'We're winnin', doctor,' it was saying exultantly. 'All along the line we're winnin' this time. The Jocks has got right away for'ard, an' the Ghurkies is in wid their killin' knives on our left. An' the Irish is in front av all. Glory be! 'Tis a big foight this time, an' it's winnin' we are. Me good arm's gone I know, but I'd rather be here wid wan arm than annywhere else wid two. An' what's an arm or a man more or less in the world? We're winnin', I tell ye--we're winnin'!'

A SMOKER'S COMPANION

Except for the address, 'No. 1, Park-lane,' marked with a muddy forefinger on the hanging waterproof sheet which served as a door, there was nothing pretentious about the erection--it could not be called a building--which was for the time being the residence of three drivers of the Royal Field Artillery. But the shelter, ingeniously constructed of hop-poles and straw thatch, was more or less rain-proof, and had the advantage of being so close to the horse-lines that half a dozen strides brought the drivers alongside their 'long-nosed chums.' It was early evening; but the horses having been watered and fed, the labours of their day were over, and the Wheel and Lead Drivers were luxuriating in bootless feet while they entertained the Gunner who had called in from his own billet in the farm's barn.

The Gunner was holding forth on Tobacco Gifts. 'It's like this, see,' he said. 'An' I knows it's so 'cos I read it myself in the paper. First you cuts a coo-pon out o' the paper wi' your name an' address on it. . . .'

'But, 'ere, 'old on,' put in the Wheel Driver. ''Ow does my name get on it?'

'You write it there, fat'ead. Didjer think it growed there? You writes your name same as the paper tells, see; an' you cuts out the coo-pon an' you sends sixpence for one packet o' 'baccy. . . .'

'Wot sorter yarn you givin' us now?' said the Wheel Driver. 'I didn't send no sixpence, or cut out a cow-pen. I gets this 'baccy for nothin'. The Quarter tole me so.'

'Course you gets it,' said the Gunner impatiently. 'But somebody must 'a' paid the sixpence. . . .'

'You said I paid it--an' I never did,' retorted the Wheel Driver.

''E means,' explained the Lead Driver, 'if you was sendin' a packet of 'baccy you'd send sixpence.'

'Where's the sense in that?' said the Wheel Driver. 'Why should I sen' sixpence when I can get this 'baccy for nothin'? I got this for nothin'. It's not a issue neither. It's a Gif'. Quartermaster tole me so.'

'We know that,' said the Gunner; 'but if you wanted to you could send sixpence. . . .'

'I could not,' said the Wheel Driver emphatically. 'I 'aven't seed a sixpence since we lef 'ome. They even pays us in bloomin' French bank notes. An' how I'm goin' to tell, after this war's over, whether my pay's in credit----'

'Oh, shut it!' interrupted the Lead Driver. 'Let's 'ear 'ow this Gift thing's worked. Go on, chum.'

'It's this way, see,' the Gunner took up his tale anew. 'S'pose you wants to send a gift . . . or mebbe you'll unnerstan' this way better. S'pose your best gel wants to sen' you a gift. . . .'

'I ain't got no bes' gel,' objected the Wheel Driver. 'I'm a married man, an' you knows it too.'

The Gunner took a deep breath and looked hard at the objector. 'Well,' he said, with studied calm, 'we'll s'pose your missis at 'ome there wants to sen' you out some smokes. . . .'

'An s'pose she *does* want to?' said the Wheel Driver truculently. 'Wot's it got to do wi' you, anyway?'

With lips pursed tight and in stony silence the Gunner glared at him, and then, turning his shoulder, addressed himself deliberately to the Lead Driver.

'S'pose *your* missis . . .' he began, but got no further.

'He ain't got no missis; leastways, 'e ain't supposed to 'ave,' the Wheel Driver interjected triumphantly.

That fact was well known to the Gunner, but had been forgotten by him in the stress of the moment. He ignored the interruption, and proceeded smoothly. 'S'pose your missis, if you 'ad one, w'ich you 'aven't, as I well knows, seein' me 'n' you walked out two sisters at Woolwich up to the larst night we was there. . . .'

The Wheel Driver chuckled.

'Thought you was on guard the las' night we was in Woolwich,' he said.

'Will you shut your 'ead an' speak when you're spoke to?' said the Gunner angrily.

'Never mind 'im, chum. Wot about this Gif' business?'

'Well,' said the Gunner, picking his words carefully. 'If a man's wife *or* gel *or* sister *or* friend wants to send 'im some smokes they cuts this coo-pon, same's I've said, an' sends it up to the paper, wi' sixpence an' the reg'mental number an' name of the man the gift's to go to. An' the paper buys the 'baccy, gettin' it cheap becos o' buyin' tons an' tons, an' sends a packet out wi the chap's number an' name and reg'ment wrote on it. So 'e gets it. An' that's all.'

The Wheel Driver could contain himself no longer. 'An' how d'you reckon I got this packet, an' no name or number on it--'cept a pos'card wi' a name an' address wrote on as I never 'eard before?'

'Becos some good-'earted bloke in Blighty[1] that doesn't 'ave no pal particular out 'ere asks the paper to send 'is packet o' 'baccy to the O.C. to pass on to some pore 'ard-up orphin Tommy that ain't got no 'baccy nor no fren's to send 'im like, an' 'e issues it to you.'

'It ain't a issue,' persisted the Wheel Driver. 'It's a Gif. The Quarter sed so 'isself.'

Splashing and squelching footsteps were heard outside, the door-curtain swung aside, and the Centre Driver ducked in, took off a soaking cap, and jerked a glistening spray off it into the darkness.

'Another fair *soor* of a night,' he remarked cheerfully, slipping out of his mackintosh and hanging the streaming garment in the door. 'Bust me if I know where all the rain comes from.'

'Any luck?' asked the Lead Driver, leaning over to rearrange the strip of cloth which, stuck in a jam-tin of fat, provided what--with some imagination--might be called a light.

'Five packets--twenty-five fags,' said the Centre Driver. 'There was two or three wantin' to swap the 'baccy in their packets for the fags in the other chaps', so I done pretty well to get five packets for mine.'

''Twould 'a' paid you better to 'ave kep' your 'baccy and made fags out o' it wi' cig'rette papers,' said the Wheel Driver.

---

1 England.

'Mebbe,' agreed the Centre Driver. 'An' p'raps you'll tell me--not being a Maskelyne an' Cook conjurer meself--'ow I'm to produce the fag-papers.'

The Gunner chuckled softly.

'You should 'a' done like old Pint-o'-Bass did, time we was on the Aisne,' he said. 'Bass is one of them fag-fiends that can't live without a cigarette, and wouldn't die happy if he wasn't smokin' one. 'E breathes more smoke than 'e does air, an' 'e ought to 'ave a permanent chimney-sweep detailed to clear the soot out of 'is lungs an' breathin' toobs. But if Pint-o'-Bass does smoke more'n is good for 'im or any other respectable factory chimney, I'll admit the smoke 'asn't sooted up 'is intelleck none, an' 'e can wriggle 'is way out of a hole where a double-jointed snake 'ud stick. An' durin' the Retreat, when, as you knows, cigarettes in the Expeditionary Force was scarcer'n snowballs in 'ell, ole Pint-o'-Bass managed to carry on, an' wasn't never seen without 'is fag, excep' at meal-times, an' sleep-times, an' they bein' so infrequent an' sketchy-like, them days, wasn't 'ardly worth countin'. 'Twas like this, see, that 'e managed it. You'll remember that, when we mobilised, some Lost Dogs' 'Ome or Society for Preventin' Christian Knowledge, or something, rushes up a issue o' pocket Testaments an' dishes out one to everybody in the Battery. Bound in a khaki cover they was, an', comin' in remarkable 'andy as a nice sentimental sort o' keepsake, most of 'em stayed be'ind wi' sweet'earts an' wives. Them as didn't must 'ave gone into "Base kit," cos any'ow there wasn't one to be raked out o' the Battery later on excep' the one that Pint-o'-Bass was carryin'. Bein' pocket Testaments, they was made o' the thinnest kind o' paper an' Bass tole me the size worked out exackly right at two fags to the page. 'E started on the Creation just about the time o' Mons, an' by the time we'd got back to the Aisne 'e was near through Genesis. All the time we was workin' up thro' France again Bass's smokes were workin' down through Exodus, an' 'e begun to worry about whether the Testament would carry 'im through the campaign. The other fellers that 'ad their tongues 'anging out for a fag uster go'n borrow a leaf off o' Bass whenever they could raise a bit o' baccy, but at last Bass shut down on these loans. "Where's your own Testament?" he'd say. "You was served out one same as me, wasn't you? Lot o' irreligious wasters! Get a Bible give you an' can't take the trouble to carry it. You'd ha' sold them Testaments at a sixpence a sack in Woolwich if there'd been buyers at that price--which there weren't. An' now you comes beggin' a page o' mine. I ain't goin' to give no more.

Encouragin' thriftlessness, as the Adjutant 'ud call it; an', besides, 'ow do I know 'ow long this war's goin' to last or when I'll see a fag or a fag-paper again? I'll be smoking Deuteronomy an' Kings long afore we're over the Rhine, an' mebbe," he sez, turnin' over the pages with 'is thumb an' tearin' out the Children of Israel careful by the roots, "mebbe I'll be reduced to smokin' the inscription, 'To our Dear Soldier Friend,' on the fly-leaf afore I gets a chance to loot some 'baccy shop in Berlin. No," 'e sez. "No. You go'n smoke a corner o' the *Pet-it Journal*, an' good enough for you, unprovident sacriligeous blighters, you--givin' away your own good Testaments."

'Young Soapy, o' the Centre Section, 'im that was struck off the strength at Wipers later through stoppin' a Coal-Box, tried to come the artful, an' 'ad the front to 'alt the Division padre one day an' ask 'im if 'e'd any spares o' pocket Testaments in store, makin' out 'e'd lost 'is through lendin' it to 'is Number One, who had gone "Missin'." Soapy made out 'e couldn't sleep in 'is bed at night--which wasn't sayin' much, seein' we mostly slep' in our seats or saddles them nights--becos 'e hadn't read a chapter o' the Testament first. An' the old sky-pilot was a little bit surprised--he'd 'a bin more surprised if 'e knew Soapy as well as I did--an' a heap pleased, and most of all bowed down wi' grief becos 'e 'adn't no Testament that was supernumary to War Establishment, and so couldn't issue one to Soapy. But two days later 'e comes 'unting for Soapy, as pleased as a dog wi' two tails, an' smilin' as glad as if 'e'd just converted the Kaiser; an' 'e lugs out a big Bible 'e'd bought in a village we'd just passed through, an' writes Soapy's name on the fly-leaf an' presents it to 'im, and tells 'im 'e'll come an' 'ave a chat any time 'e's near the Battery. The Bible was none o' your fiddlin' pocket things, but a good substantial one, wi' pitchers o' Moses in the bulrushes an' Abraham scarifyin' 'is son, an' such like. An' the leaves was that thick that Soapy might as well 'ave smoked brown paper or the *Pet-it Journal*. But that wasn't the worst of it. Soapy chucked it over the first 'edge soon as the padre 'ad gone, but next day the padre rolls up and tells Soapy a Sapper 'ad picked it up and brought it to 'im--'im 'avin' signed 'is name an' rank after "Presented by----" on the fly-leaf. An' 'e warns Soapy to be more careful, and 'elps 'im stow it in 'is 'aversack, where it took up most the room an' weighed a ton, an' left Soapy to distribute 'is bully beef an' biscuits an' cheese an' spare socks and cetera in all the pockets 'e 'ad. An even then poor Soapy wasn't finished, for every time the padre got a chance 'e'd 'op round an' 'ave a chat, as 'e called it, wi' Soapy, the chat being a cross-examination worse'n a Court-Martial on what chapter Soapy 'ad been readin,' an' full explanations of same. Soapy was drove at last to readin' a chapter, so 'e could make out 'e savvied something of it.'

The Gunner tapped out his pipe on the heel of his boot and began to re-fill it.

'If you'll believe me,' he said, 'that padre got poor Soapy pinned down so he was readin' near a chapter a day--which shows the 'orrible results that can come o' a little bit of simple deception.'

'An' how is Pint-o'-Bass goin' on wi' his Testament?' asked the Lead Driver.

"E don't need to smoke it, now we're in these fixed positions an' getting liberal supplies from these people that sends up to the papers' Tobacco Funds. But 'e's savin' up the rest of it. Reckons that when we get the Germans on the run again the movin' will be at the trot canter an' gallop, same's before; an' the cigarette supplies won't be able to keep up the pace. An' besides, 'e sez, 'e reckons it's only a fair thing to smoke a cig'rette made wi' the larst chapter down the 'Igh Street o' Berlin the day Peace is declared.'

THE JOB OF THE AM. COL.

The wide door of the barn creaked open and admitted a swirl of sleety snow, a gust of bitter cold wind, and the Bombardier. A little group of men round a guttering candle-lamp looked up.

'Hello, Father Christmas,' said the Centre Driver. 'You're a bit late for your proper day, but we'll let you off that if you fill our stockin's up proper.'

'Wipe yer feet careful on the mat,' said the Lead Driver, 'an' put yer umbrella in the 'all stand.'

''Ere, don't go shakin' that snow all over the straw,' said the Wheel Driver indignantly. 'I'm goin' to sleep there presently an' the straw's damp enough as it is.'

'Glad you're so sure about sleepin' there,' the Bombardier said, divesting himself of his bandolier and struggling out of his snow-covered coat. 'By the look o' things, it's quite on the cards you get turned out presently an' have to take up some pills to the guns.'

'Pretty busy to-night, ain't they?' said the Centre Driver. 'We heard 'em bumpin' away good-oh.'

'You don't 'ear the 'alf of it back 'ere,' said the Bombardier. 'Wind's blowin' most o' the row away. They're goin' it hot an' strong. Now where's my mess-tin got to? 'Aven't 'ad no tea yet, an' it's near eight o'clock. I'm just about froze through too.'

'Here y'are,' said the Centre Driver, throwing a mess-tin over. 'An' the cook kep' tea hot for you an' the rest that was out.'

'Pull that door shut be'ind you,' said the Wheel Driver. 'This barn's cold as a ice-'ouse already, an' the roof leaks like a broke sieve. Billet! Strewth, it ain't 'arf a billet!'

The Bombardier returned presently with a mess-tin of 'raw' (milkless and sugarless) tea and proceeded to make a meal off that, some stone-hard biscuits and the scrapings of a pot of jam.

'What sort o' trip did you 'ave?' asked the Centre Driver. 'Anyways peaceful, or was you dodgin' the Coal-Boxes this time?'

'Not a Coal-Box, or any other box,' said the Bombardier, hammering a biscuit to fragments with a rifle-butt. 'An' I 'aven't 'ad a shell drop near me for a week.'

'If we keeps on like this,' said the Centre Driver, 'we'll get fancyin' we're back on Long Valley man-oovers.'

'Wot you grousin' about anyway?' remarked the Wheel Driver. 'This is a Ammunition Column, ain't it? Or d'you s'pose it's an Am. Col.'s bizness to go chasin' after bombardments an' shell-fire. If you ain't satisfied you'd better try'n get transferred to the trenches.'

'Or if that's too peaceful for you,' put in the Lead Driver, 'you might apply to be sent to England where the war's ragin' an' the Zeppelins is killin' wimmin an' window-panes.'

'Talkin' o' transferring to the trenches,' said the Bombardier putting down his empty mess-tin and producing his pipe. 'Reminds me o' a Left'nant we 'ad join us a month or two back. It was the time you chaps was away attached to that other Division, so you didn't know 'im. 'E'd bin with a Battery right through, but 'e got a leave an' when 'e come back from England 'e was sent to us. 'Is batman[2] tole me 'e was a bit upset at first about bein' cut adrift from 'is pals in the Battery but 'e perked up an' reckoned 'e was goin' to 'ave things nice an' cushy for a bit. An' 'e as much as says so himself to me the first time 'e was takin' ammunition up an' I was along with 'im. I'd been doin' orderly at the Battery an' brought down the requisition for so many rounds, an' it bein' the Left'nant's first trip up, an' not knowin' the road 'e 'as me up in front with 'im to show the way. It was an unusual fine mornin' I remember, 'avin' stopped rainin' for almost an hour, an' just as we started somethin' that might 'ave been a sun tried 'is 'ardest to shine. Soon as we was on the road the Left'nant gives the word to march at ease, an' lights up a cig'rette 'imself.

'"Great mornin' ain't it, Bombardier?" 'e sez. "Not more'n a foot or two o' mud on the roads, an' the temperature almost above freezin'-point. I'm just about begin-

2 Servant.

nin' to like this job on the Am. Col. 'Ave you bin with a Battery out 'ere?"

'I tole 'im yes an' came to the Column after bein' slightly wounded.

"'Well," 'e sez, "you knows 'ow much better off you are 'ere. You don't 'ave no standin' to the gun 'arf the night in the rain, an' live all the rest o' the nights an' all the days in a dirty, muddy, stuffy funk-'ole. That's the one thing I'm most glad to be out of," 'e sez. "Livin' under the ground, like a rabbit in a burrow with every chance of 'avin' 'is 'ead blowed off if 'e looks up over the edge. I've 'ad enough o' dug-outs an' observin' from the trenches, an' Coal-Box dodgin' to last me a bit, an' it's a pleasant change to be ridin' a decent 'orse on a most indecent apology for a road, an' not a Jack Johnson in sight, even if they are in 'earing."

"'E made several more remarks like that durin' the mornin', an' of course I agreed with 'im. I mostly does agree with an officer an' most especial a young 'un. If you don't, 'e always thinks 'e's right an' you're just that much big a fool not to know it. An' the younger 'e is, the more right 'e is, an' the bigger fool you or anyone else is.

'Well, the Left'nant's enthoosy-ism cools off a bit when it begins to rain again like as if some one had turned on the tap o' a waterfall, but he tried to cheer himself remarkin' that most likely 'is Battery was bein' flooded out of their dug-outs. But I could see he was beginnin' to doubt whether the Am. Col.'s job was as cushy as he'd reckoned when the off-lead o' Number One wagon tries a cross-Channel-swim act in one of them four-foot deep ditches. The wagons 'ad to pull aside to let some transport motor-lorries past an' One's off-lead that was a new 'orse just come to the Column from Base Remounts an' had some objections to motor-lorries hootin' in his ear an' scrapin' past a eighth of an inch from his nose--'e side-slipped into the ditch. 'E stood there wi' the water up to 'is shoulder an' the lead driver lookin' down on 'im an' repeatin' rapid-fire prayers over 'im. I may say it took the best bit o' half an hour to get that blighter on to the road again an' the Left'nant prancin' round an' sayin' things a parrot would blush to repeat. But 'e did more than say things, an' I'm willin' to admit it. 'E got down off his horse an' did 'is best to coax the off-lead out wi' kind words an' a ridin' cane. An' when they missed fire an' we got a drag-rope round the silly brute the Left'nant laid 'old an' muddied himself up wi' the rest. We 'ad to dig down the bank a bit at last an' hook a team on the drag-rope, an' we pulled that 'orse out o' the mud like pullin' a cork from a bottle. It was rainin' in tons all this time an' I fancy the Left'nant's opinion o' the Am. Col.'s job had reined back another pace or two, especially as he'd slipped an' come down full length in the mud when haulin' on the drag-rope, an' had also slid one leg in the ditch well over the boot-top in reachin' out for a good swipe wi' the cane.

'We plods off again at last, an' presently we begins to get abreast o' some position where one o' our big siege guns was beltin' away. A bit further on, the road took a turn an' the siege gun's shells were roarin' along over our heads like an express train goin' through a tunnel; an' the Left'nant kept cockin' a worried eye round every time she banged an' presently 'e sez sharp-like to the drivers to walk out their teams and get clear of the line of fire.

'"If a German battery starts trying to out that feller," he sez to me, "we just about stand a healthy chance of meetin' an odd shell or two that's tryin' for the range."

'We had to pass through a bit of a town called Palloo,[3] an' just before we comes to it we met some teams from one of the Column's other sections comin' back. Their officer was in front an' as we passed he called to the Left'nant that Palloo had been shelled that mornin' an' the Headquarter Staff near blotted out.

'I could just see the Left'nant chewin' this over as we went on, an' presently he asks me if it's anyways a frequent thing for us to come under fire takin' ammunition up. I told 'im about a few o' the times I'd seen it happen myself, an' also about how we had the airmen an' the German guns makin' a dead set at the Column durin' the Retreat an' shellin' us out o' one place after the other.

'Before I finished it we hears the whoop o' a big shell an' a crash in the town, an' the drivers begins to look round at each other. Bang-bang another couple o' shells drops in poor old Palloo, an' the drivers begins to look at the Left'nant an' to finger their reins. He kep' on, an' of course I follows 'im an' the teams follows us.

'"I see there's a church tower in the town, Bombardier," he sez. "Does our road run near it?"

'I told him we 'ad to go through the square where the church stood.

3   The identity of the town is very effectually placed beyond recognition by the Bombardier's pronunciation.

'"Then we come pretty near walkin' through the bull's-eye o' their target," he sez; "for I'll bet they're reckonin' on an observation post bein' in the tower, an' they're tyin' to out it."

'We got into Palloo an' it was like goin' through it at midnight, only wi' day-light instead of lamp-light. There wasn't an inhabitant to be seen, except one man peepin' up from a cellar gratin', an' one woman runnin' after a toddlin' kid that 'ad strayed out. She was shriekin' quick-fire French at it an' when she grabbed it up an' started back the kid opened 'is lungs an' near yelled the roof off. The woman ran into a house an' the door slammed an' shut off the shriekin' like liftin' the needle off a gramaphone disc. An' it left the main street most awful empty an' still wi' the jingle o' the teams' harness an' clatter o' the wagon wheels the only sounds. Anoth-er few shells came in an' one hit a house down the street in front of us. We saw the slates an' the chimney pots fair jump in the air an' the 'ole 'ouse sort of collapsed in a heap an' a billowin' cloud o' white smoke an' dust. There was some of our troops hookin' a few wounded civilians out as we passed and the road was cluttered up wi' bricks an' half a door an' broken bits o' chairs an' tables an' crockery. Fair blew the inside out o' the house, that shell did.

'When we come clear o' the town there was a long stretch o' clear road to cover, an' we was ploddin' down this when we hears the hum o' an airyplane. The Left'nant squints up an' "It's a Tawb," he sez.

'"Beggin' your pardon sir," I told 'im, "but it's a German. No mistakin' them bird-shaped wings an' tail. He's a German, sure enough."

'"That's what I just said, Bombardier," he sez, which it wasn't but I knew it was no use sayin' so.

'The airyplane swoops round an' comes flyin' straight to us an' passed about our heads an' circles round to have a good look at us. The Left'nant was fair riled.

'"Dash 'is impidence," he sez. "If he'd only come a bit lower we might fetch him a smack"; an' he tells the gunners to get their rifles out. But the German knew too much to come close down though he flew right over us once or twice.

'"Why in thunder don't some of our guns have a whale at 'im,'" the Left'nant says angry-like, "'or our airmen get up an' shoot some holes in 'im. He'll be droppin' a clothes-basketful o' bombs on my wagons presently, like as not. An' I can't even loose off a rifle at the bounder. Good Lord, that ever I should live to walk along a road like a tame sheep an' let a mouldy German chuck parcels o' bombs at me without me being able to do more'n shake my fist at 'im. . . ." 'An he swore most vicious. The airyplane flew off at last but even then the Left'nant wasn't satisfied. "He'll be off back 'ome to report this Ammunition Column on this particular spot on the road," he sez, "if he's not tickin' off the glad tidings on a wireless to 'is batteries now. An' presently I suppose they'll start starring this road wi' high-explosive shell. Did ever you know a wagon full to the brim wi' lyddite being hit by a high-explosive, Bombardier, or hear how 'twould affect the Column's health?"

'"I knew of a German column that one of our airyplanes dropped a bomb on, at the Aisne, sir," I sez. "I passed the place on the road myself soon after."

'"An' what happened?" he asks, an' I told 'im it seemed the bomb exploded the wagon it hit an' the wagons exploded each other. "That Ammunition Column," I sez, "went off like a packet o' crackers, one wagon after the other. An' when we came up, all that was left o' that column was a reek o' sulphur an' a hole in the road."

'"That's cheerful," sez the Left'nant. "With us loaded down to the gunn'l wi' lyddite, an' the prospect o' being a target for every German gun within range o' this road." He fidgeted in his saddle a bit, an' then, "I suppose," he sez, "they'll calculate our pace an' the distance we've moved since this airman saw us, an' they'll shell the section o' road just ahead of us now to glory. I'd halt for a bit just to cheat 'em, for they'll shoot by the map without seein' us. But that requisition for lyddite was urgent, wasn't it?"

'I told him it was so, an' the Battery captain had told me to get it in quick to the column.

'"Then we'll just have to push on an' chance it," sez the Left'nant, "though I must own I do hate being made a helpless runnin'-deer target to every German gunner that likes to coco-nut shy at me. . . . Like a packet o' crackers. . . . Good Lord!"

'We plodded on, the Left'nant spurrin' his horse on and reinin' him back, an' cockin' his ear for the first shell bumpin' on the road. Nothin' happened for quite a bit after that, an' I was just about beginnin' to feel satisfied that the Germ bird 'ad run into a streak o' air that our anti-aircraft guns kept strickly preserved an' that they'd served a Trespassers-will-be-Spiflicated notice on 'im an' had punctured him an' his wings. But just as we rounded a curve an' came into a long straight piece o' the road, I hears a high-risin' swoosh an' before it finished an' before the bang o' the burst reached us, spout goes a cloud o' black smoke 'way far down the road.'

'"This," says the Left'nant, "is goin' to be highly interestin', not to say excitin', presently. I figure that's either a four-point-two or a five-point-nine-inch high-explosive Hun. An' there's another o' the dose from the same bottle, an' about a hundred yards this way along the road. I dunno how their high-explosive will mix wi' ours, but if they get one direct hit on a wagon we'll know all about it pretty quick. A Brock's Crystal Palace firework show won't be in it wi' the ensooin' performance. An' that remark o' yours, bombardier, about a packet o' crackers recurs to my min' wi' most disquietin' persistency. 'An' still they come,' as the poet remarks."

'They was comin' too, an' no fatal error. No hurry about 'em, but a most alarmin' regularity. They was all pitchin' plumb on that road, an' each one about fifty to a hundred yards nearer our procession, an' us walkin' straight into the shower too. The swoosh-bang o' each one kep' gettin' louder an' louder, an' not a single one was missin' the road. I tell you, I could feel the flesh creepin' on my bones an' a feelin' in the pit o' my stomach like I'd swallowed a tuppenny ice-cream whole. There was no way o' dodgin', remember. We'd a ditch lippin' full o' water along both sides o' the road an' we knew without lookin'--though the Left'nant did 'ave one squint--that they was the usual brand o' ditch hereabouts, anythin' down to six foot deep an' sides cut down as straight as a cellar wall. It was no use trottin' 'cos we might just be hurryin' up to be in time to arrive on the right spot to meet one. An' it was no use haltin' for exactly the same reason. The Left'nant reins back beside the leadin' team, an' believe me there wasn't one pair o' eyes in all that outfit that wasn't glued on 'im nor a pair o' ears that wasn't waitin' anxious for some order to come, an' I'm includin' my own eyes an' ears in the catalogue. There was nothin' to be done an' nothin' to be said, an' we all knew it, but at the same time we was ready to jump to any order the Left'nant passed out. The shells was droppin' at about ten to fifteen seconds' interval, an' we could see it was goin' to be a matter o' blind luck whether one pitched short or over or fair a-top o' us. They were closer spaced, too, as they come nearer, an' I reckon there wasn't more'n fifty or sixty yards atween the last two or three bursts. An' we was still walkin' on, every man wi' his reins short an' feelin' 'is 'orse's mouth, an' his knees grippin' the saddle hard.

"'Bang!" one hits the road about one-fifty to two hundred yards short an' we heard chips o' it whizz an' hum past us. The Left'nant looks, round. "When I say 'trot' you'll trot," he shouts, "an' no man is to stop or slow up to pick up anyone hit."

'Next second, "Crash!" comes another about a hundred yards off, an' before the lumps of it sung past, "Ter-r-rot!" yells the Left'nant. Now some people might call the en-sooin' movement a trot, an' some might call it a warm canter an' first cousin to a gallop. We sees the game in a wink--to get past the spot the next crump was due to arrive on afore it did arrive. We did it too--handsome an' wi' some to spare, though when I heard the roarin' swoosh of it comin' down I thought we was for it an' a direck hit was due. But it went well over an' none of the splinters touched.

"'Steady there, steady," shouts the Left'nant "but keep goin'. They'll repeat the series if they've any sense." We could hear the blighters crumpin' away back down the road behind us, an' believe me we kep' goin' all right. But the Boshe didn't repeat the series; he went on a new game an' just afore we came to the end o' the straight stretch four crumps pitched down astride the road ahead of us about two hundred yards. One hit the edge o' the road an' the others in the fields on both sides an' one of these was a dud an' didn't burst. But we knew that the fellers that did go off would make a highly unhealthy circle around an' the prospect o' being there or thereabouts when the next boo-kay landed wasn't none too allurin'. The Left'nant yells to come on, an' we came, oh, take it from me, we came a-humpin'. There was some fancy driving past them crump holes in the road, but we might have been at Olympia the way them drivers shaved past at the canter. We was just past the last spot the four landed when I heard the whistle o' another bunch comin' an' my hair near lifted my cap off. Them wagons o' ours isn't built for any speed records but I fancy they covered more ground in the next few seconds than ever they've done before. But goin' our best, there was no hope o' clearin' the blast o' the explosions if they explosioned on the same target, an' we all made ourselves as small as we could on our horses' backs an' felt we was as big as a barn all the time the rush was gettin' louder an' louder. Then thud-thud-thud an' crash! three of 'em dropped blind an' only the one exploded; an' it bein' in the ditch didn't do any harm beyond sendin' up a spout o' water about a mile high. Three duds out o' four--if that wasn't a miracle I want to know. But we wasn't countin' too much on it bein' miracle day an' we kept the wheels goin' round with the whistle over-'ead an' the crashes behind to discourage any loiterin' to gather flowers by the way.

'An' when we was well past an' slowed down again I heard the Left'nant draw a deep breath an' say soft-like ". . . a packet o' Chinese crackers."

'But 'e said something stronger that same night. He'd just crawled back to the Column wi' his empty wagons leavin' me as orderly at the Battery, an' me havin' a pressin' message to take back for more shells I trotted out an' got back soon after he did. I took my message to the old farm where the officers was billeted an' the mess-man takes my note in. I got a glimpse o' the Left'nant wi' his jacket an' boots off an' his breeches followin' suit. "I'd a rotten day," he was sayin', "but one good point about this Am. Col. job--an' the only one I see--is that you get the night in bed wi' your breeches off."

'But if you'd only 'eard 'im when he found he was for the road again at once an' would spend 'is night in the rain an' dark instead of in bed--well, I couldn't repeat 'is language, not 'aving the talent to 'is extent.

''E was transferred to a battery soon after an' I 'eard that when he got the orders all 'e 'ad to say was, "Thank 'Eaven. I'll mebbe get shelled oftener in a battery, but at least I'll 'ave the satisfaction o' shellin' back--an' *I may* 'ave a funk-hole handy to duck in when it's extry hot, instead o' ridin' on the road an' expectin' to go off like a packet 'o crackers."

'Mebbe he was right,' concluded the Bombardier reflectively. 'But I s'pose it's entirely a matter o' taste, an' how a man likes bein' killed off.'

THE SIGNALLER'S DAY

The gun detachment were curled up and dozing on the damp straw of their dug-out behind the gun when the mail arrived. The men had had an early turn-out that morning, had been busy serving or standing by the gun all day, and had been under a heavy shell fire off and on for a dozen hours past. As a result they were fairly tired--the strain and excitement of being under fire are even more physically exhausting somehow than hard bodily labour--and might have been hard to rouse. But the magic words 'The mail' woke them quicker than a round of gun-fire, and they sat up and rubbed the sleep from their eyes and clustered eagerly round the Number One (sergeant in charge of the detachment) who was 'dishing out' the letters. Thereafter a deep silence fell on the dug-out, the recipients of letters crowding with bent heads round the guttering candle, the disappointed ones watching them with envious eyes.

An exclamation of deep disgust from the Signaller brought no comment until the last letter was read, but then the Limber Gunner remembered and remarked on it.

'What was that you was rearin' up an' snortin' over, Signals?' he asked, carefully retrieving a cigarette stump from behind his ear and lighting up.

The Signaller snorted again. 'Just 'ark at this,' he said, unfolding his letter again. 'I'll just read this bit, an' then I'll tell you the sort of merry dance I've 'ad to-day. This is from an uncle o' mine in London. 'E grouses a bit about the inconvenience o' the dark streets, an' then 'e goes on, "Everyone at 'ome is wonderin' why you fellows don't get a move on an' do somethin'. The official despatches keeps on sayin' 'no movement,' or 'nothin' to report,' or 'all quiet,' till it looks as if you was all asleep. Why don't you get up an' go for 'em?"'

The Signaller paused and looked up. 'See?' he said sarcastically. 'Everyone at 'ome is wonderin', an' doesn't like this "all quiet" business. I wish everyone at 'ome, including this uncle o' mine, 'ad been up in the trenches to-day.'

'Have a lively time?' asked the Number One. 'We had some warmish spells back here. They had the range to a dot, and plastered us enthusiastic with six- an' eight-inch Johnsons an' H.E. shrapnel. We'd three wounded an' lucky to get off so light.'

'Lively time's the right word for my performance,' said the Signaller. 'Nothin' of the "all quiet" touch in my little lot to-day. It started when we was goin' up at daybreak--me an' the other telephonist wi' the Forward Officer. You know that open stretch of road that takes you up to the openin' o' the communication trenches? Well, we're just nicely out in the middle o' that when Fizz comes a shell an' Bang just over our 'eads, an' the shrapnel rips down on the road just behind us. Then Bang-Bang-Bang they come along in a reg'lar string down the road. They couldn't see us, an' I suppose they was just shooting on the map in the hopes o' catching any reliefs o' the infantry on the road. Most o' the shells was percussion, after the first go, an' they was slam-bangin' down in the road an' the fields alongside an' flinging dirt and gravel in showers over us. "Come on," sez the Forward Officer; "this locality is lookin' unhealthy," an' we picked up our feet an' ran for it. Why we wasn't all killed about ten times each I'll never understand; but we wasn't, an' we got to the end o' the communication trench an' dived into it as thankful as any rabbit that ever reached 'is burrow with a terrier at 'is tail. After we got a bit o' breath back we ploughed along the trench--it was about ankle deep in bits--to the Infantry Headquarters, an' the F.O. goes inside. After a bit 'e comes out an' tells me to come on wi' him up to the Observation Post. This was about eight ac emma [A.M.], an' just gettin' light enough to see. You know what that Observin' Post of ours is. The F.O. 'as a fond de-looshun that the Germs can't see you when you leave the support trench an' dodge up the wreckage of that hedge to the old house; but I 'ave my own opinions about it. Anyway I've never been up yet without a most unnatural lot o' bullets chippin' twigs off the hedge an' smackin' into the ditch. But we got into the house all right an' I unslings my Telephone--Portable--D Mark III., an' connects up with the Battery while the F. O. crawls up into the top storey. 'E hadn't been there three minutes when smack . . . smack, I hears two bullets hit the tiles or the walls. The F. O. comes down again in about ten minutes an' has a talk to the Major at the Battery. He reports fairly quiet except some Germ Pip-Squeak shells droppin' out on our right, an' a good deal o' sniping rifle fire between the trenches in front of us. As a general thing I've no serious objection to the trenches snipin' each other, if only the Germs 'ud aim more careful. But mostly they aims shockin' an' anything that comes high for our trench just has the right elevation for our post. There's a broken window on the ground floor too, lookin' out of the room we uses straight at the Boshies, an' the F.O. wouldn't have me block this up at no price. "Concealment," sez he, "is better than protection. An' if they see that window sandbagged up it's a straight tip to them this is a Post of some sort, an' a hearty invitation to them to plunk a shell or two in on us." Maybe 'e was right, but you can't well conceal a whole house or even the four walls o' one, so I should 'ave voted for the protection myself. Anyhow, 'e said I could build a barricade at the foot o' the stairs, where I'd hear him call 'is orders down, an' I'd be behind some cover. This motion was seconded by a bullet comin' in the window an' puttin' a hole in the eye o' a life-size enlargement photo of an old lady in a poke-bonnet hangin' on the wall opposite. The row of the splinterin' glass made me think a Jack Johnson had arrived an' I didn't waste time gettin' to work on my barricade. I got a arm-chair an' the half of a sofa an' a broken-legged table, an' made that the foundation; an' up against the outside of them I stacked a lot o' table linen an' books an' loose bricks an' bottles an' somebody's Sunday clothes an' a fender an' fire-irons an' anything else I thought any good to turn a bullet. I finished up by prizin' up a hearthstone from the fireplace an' proppin' it up against the back o' the arm-chair an' sittin' down most luxurious in the chair an' lighting up my pipe. That's a long ways the most comfort-able chair I've ever sat in--deep soft springy seat an' padded arms an' covered in red velvet--an' I was just thinkin' what a treat it was when I hears the rifle fire out in front beginnin' to brisk up, an' the Forward Officer calls down to me to warn the Battery to stand by because o' some excitement in the trenches. "Major says would you like him to give them a few rounds, sir," I shouts up, an' the F.O. says, "Yes-- three rounds gun-fire, on the lines the guns are laid." So off goes your three rounds, an' I could hear your shells whoopin' along over our heads.

"'Number One gun add twenty-five yards," calls down the F.O., an' then gives some more corrections an' calls for one round battery fire. By this time the rifle fire out in front was pretty thick and the bullets was hissin' an' whinin' past us an' crackin' on the walls. Another one came through the window an' perforated the old lady's poke-bonnet, but none o' them was comin' near me, an' I was just about happily concludin' I wasn't in the direct line o' fire an' was well covered from strays. So I was snuggin' down in my big easy chair with the D Mark III. on my knee, puffin' my pipe an' repeatin' the F.O.'s orders as pleasant as you please when crack! a bullet comes with an almighty smack through the back o' the arm-chair, bare inches off my ear. Comfort or no comfort, thinks I, this is where I resign the chair, an' I slides out an' squats well down on the wet floor. It's surprisin' too the amount o' wet an ordinary carpet can hold, an' the chap that designed the pattern o' this one might 'ave worked in some water lilies an' duckweed instead o' red roses an' pink leaves if he'd known 'ow it would come to be used. This 'ouse 'as been rather a swagger one, judgin' by the style o' the furniture, but one end an' the roof 'aving gone west with the shellin' the whole show ain't what it might be. An' when the missus as it belongs to returns to 'er 'appy 'ome there's going to be some fervent remarks passed about the Germs an' the war generally.

'But to get on wi' the drill--the row in the trenches got hotter an' hotter, an' our house might 'ave been a high-power magnet for bullets, the way they was comin' in, through that open window special. The old lady lost another eye an' half an' ear, an' 'er Sunday gown an' a big gold brooch was shot to ribbons. A bullet cut the cord at last, an' the old girl came down bump. But I'd been watchin' 'er so long I felt she oughtn't to be disgraced lyin' there on 'er face before the German fire. So I crawled out an' propped 'er up against the wall with 'er face to the window. I 'ope she'd be glad to know 'er photo went down with flyin' poke-bonnet.'

'It was shortly after this our wire was first cut--about ten ac emma [A.M.] that would be. I sings out to the F.O. that I was disc[4], but what wi' the bullets smackin' into the walls, the shells passin' over us, the Coal-Boxes bursting around, an' the trenches belting off at their hardest, the F.O. didn't 'ear me an' I 'ad to crawl up the stairs to 'im. Just as I got to the top a shrap burst, an' the bullets came smashin' an' tearin' down thro' the tiles an' rafters. The bullets up there was whistlin' an' whinin' past an' over like the wind in a ship's riggin', an' every now an' then ***whack!*** one would hit a tile, sending the dust an' splinters jumpin'. The F.O. was crouched

---

4 Disconnected.

up in one corner where a handful o' tiles was still clingin', an' he was peepin' out through these with 'is field glasses. "Keep down," 'e sez when 'e saw me. "There's a brace o' blanky snipers been tryin' for a cold 'alf-hour to bull's-eye on to me. There they go again----," an' ***crack . . . smack*** two bullets comes, one knockin' another loose tile off, a foot over 'is 'ead, an' t'other puttin' a china ornament on the mantel-piece on the casualty list.

'I reported the wire cut an' the F.O. sez he'd come along wi' me an' locate the break. "We'll have to hurry," he says, "cos it looks to me as if a real fight was breezin' up." So we crawled out along the ditch an' down the trench, followin' the wire. We found the break--there was three cuts--along that bit o' road that runs from the Rollin' River Trench down past the Bomb Store, an' I don't ever want a more highly excitin' job than we had mendin' it. The shells was fair rainin' down that road, an' the air was just hummin' like a harpstring wi' bullets an' rickos.[5] We joined up an' tapped in an' found we was through all right, so we hustled back to the Post. That 'ouse never was a real 'ealth resort, but today it was suthin' wicked. They must 'ave suspicioned there was a Post there, an' they kep' on pastin' shells at us. How they missed us so often, Heaven an' that German gunner only knows. They couldn't get a direct with solid, but I must admit they made goodish shootin' wi' shrapnel, an' they've made that 'ouse look like a second-'and pepper-caster. The F.O. was 'avin' a most unhappy time with shrapnel an' rifle bullets, but 'e 'ad 'is guns in action, so 'e just 'ad to stick it out an' go on observin', till the wires was cut again. This time the F.O. sez to look back as far as the wire ran in the trench, an' if I didn't find the break up to there come back an' report to 'im. But I found the break in the hedge jus' outside, an' mended it an' went back, the bullets still zipping down an' me breakin' all the hands-an'-knees records for the fifty yards. I found the F.O. 'ad reined back a bit from 'is corner an' was busy wi' the bedroom poker breakin' out a loophole through the bricks of the gable-end wall. 'E came down an' told the Major about it. It was getting too hot, 'e said, an' the two snipers must 'ave 'im located wi' field-glasses. One bullet 'ad nearly blinded 'im wi' broken-tile dust, an' another 'ad tore a hole across the side of 'is "British warm"[6]; so he was goin' to try observin' through a couple of loopholes. Then 'e went up an' finished 'is chippin' an' brought the guns into action again. Just in the middle o' a series I feels a most unholy crash,

5   Ricochets.
6   Overcoat.

an' the whole house rocked on its toe an' heel. The brickdust an' plaster came rattlin' down, an' when the dust cleared a bit an' I got my sense an' my eyesight back, I could see a splintered hole in the far corner of my ceilin'. I made sure the F.O. upstairs was blotted out, 'cos it was that corner upstairs where 'is loophole was; but next minute 'e sings out an' asks was I all right. I never felt less all right in my life, but I told 'im I was still alive, far as knew. I crawled up to see what 'ad 'appened, an' there was 'im in one corner at 'is peep-'ole, an' the floor blowed to splinters behind 'im an' a big gap bust in the gable wall at the other corner. A shell had made a fair hit just about on 'is one loophole, while he was lookin' thro' the other. "I believe we'll 'ave to leave this," he sez, "an' move along to our other post. It's a pity, 'cos I can't see near as well."

'"If we don't leave this 'ouse, sir," I sez, "seems to me it'll leave us--an' in ha'penny numbers at that."

'So he reports to the Major, an' I packs up, an' we cleared. The shelling had slacked off a bit, though the trenches was still slingin' lead hard as ever.

'"We must hurry," sez the F.O. "They're going to bombard a trench for ten minutes at noon, and I must be in touch by then."

'We scurried round to the other post, and just got fixed up before the shoot commenced. And in the middle of it--phutt goes first one wire an' then the other. The F.O. said things out loud when I told him. "Come along," he finished up; "we must mend it at once. The infantry assault a trench at the end of the ten minutes. There they go now," and we heard the roar of the rifles swell up again. He took a long stare out through his glasses and then we doubled out. The Germs must have thought there was a big assault on, and their gunners were putting a zone of fire behind the trenches to stop supports coming up. An' we had to go through that same zone, if you please. 'Strewth, it was hot. There was big shells an' little shells an' middle-sized shells, roarin' an' shrieking up and bursting H.E. shrapnel or smashing into the ground. If there was one threw dirt over us there was a dozen. One buzzed close past and burst about twenty feet in front of the F.O., and either the windage or the explosion lifted him off his feet and clean rolled him over. I thought he was a goner again, but when I came up to him he was picking himself up, an' spittin' dirt an' language out between his teeth, an' none the worse except for the shakin'. We couldn't find that break. We had to tap in all along the wire to locate it and all the time it was a race between us finding the break and a shell finding us. At last we got it, where we'd run the wire over a broke-up shed. The F.O. was burnin' to talk to the Battery, knowing they'd be anxious about their shoot, so he picked a spot in the lee of a wall an' told me to tap in on the wire there. Just as he began talkin' to the Battery a Coal-Box soars up an' bumps down about twenty yards away and beyond us. The F.O. looks up, but goes on talkin'; but when another shell, an' then another, drops almost on the exact same spot, he lifted the 'phone closer in to the wall and stoops well down to it. I needn't tell you I was down as close to the ground as I could get without digging. "I think we're all right here," sez the F.O., when another shell bust right on the old spot an' the splinters went singin' over us. "They look like keepin' on the same spot, and we must be out of the line the splinters take."

'It looked like he was right, for about three more fell without touchin' us, and I was feeling a shade easier in my mind. There was some infantry comin' up on their way to the support trenches, an' they filed along by the wall that was coverin' us. Just as they was passin' another shell dropped. It was on the same spot as all the others, but blow me if it didn't get three of them infantry. They fell squirmin' right on top o' us an' the instrument, so I concluded that spot wasn't as safe as the F.O. had reckoned, an' there was a flaw in 'is argument somewheres that the Coal-Box 'ad found out. The F.O. saw that too, an' we shifted out quick-time. After that things quietened down a bit, an' the short hairs on the back o' my neck had time to lie down. They stood on end again once or twice in the afternoon, when we'd some more repairin' under fire to do; an' then to wind up the day they turned a maxim on just as we was comin' away from the post, an' we had to flop on our faces with the bullets zizz-izz-ipping just over us. We took a trench, I hear; an' the Jocks in front of us had thirty casualties, and the Guards on our left 'ad some more, 'cos I seed 'em comin' back to the ambulance.

'On the 'ole, it's been about the most unpleasantest day I've spent for a spell. What wi' wadin' to the knees in the trench mud, getting soaked through wi' rain, not 'aving a decent meal all day, crawlin' about in mud an' muck, an' gettin' chiv-vied an' chased all over the landscape wi' shells an' shrapnel an' machine-guns an' rifles, I've just about 'ad enough o' this King an' Country game.'

The Signaller paused a moment. But his gaze fell on the letter he still held in his hand, and he tapped it with a scornful finger and burst out again violently: 'King an' Country--huh! An' a bald-'eaded blighter sittin' warm an' dry an' comfortable by 'is fireside at 'ome writes out an' tells me what the Country's thinkin'. I come in 'ere after a day that's enough to turn the 'air of a 'earse-'orse grey, an' I'm told about my pals bein' casualtied; an' to top it all I gets a letter from 'ome--"why don't you do somethin'? Why don't you get up an' go for 'em?" Ar-r-rh!!'

''Ome,' remarked the Limber Gunner. ''Ome don't know nuthin' about it.'

'They don't,' agreed the Signaller. 'But what I wants to know--an' there's a many 'ere like me--is why don't somebody let 'em know about it; let 'em really know.'

www.bookjungle.com *email: sales@bookjungle.com fax: 630-214-0564 mail: Book Jungle PO Box 2226 Champaign, IL 61825*

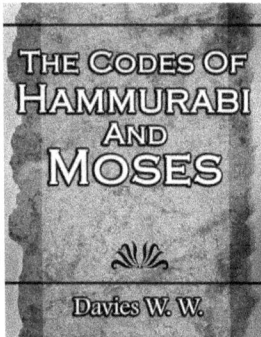

The Codes Of Hammurabi And Moses
W. W. Davies

QTY

The discovery of the Hammurabi Code is one of the greatest achievements of archaeology, and is of paramount interest, not only to the student of the Bible, but also to all those interested in ancient history...

Religion   **ISBN:** *1-59462-338-4*   **Pages:132**
MSRP $12.95

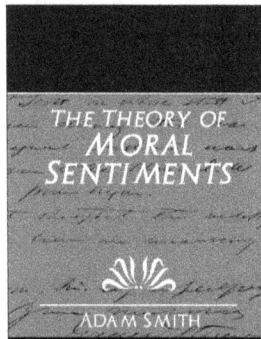

The Theory of Moral Sentiments
Adam Smith

QTY

This work from 1749. contains original theories of conscience amd moral judgment and it is the foundation for systemof morals.

Philosophy **ISBN:** *1-59462-777-0*   **Pages:536**
MSRP $19.95

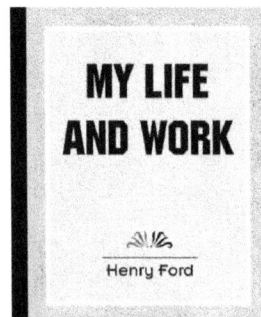

Jessica's First Prayer
Hesba Stretton

QTY

In a screened and secluded corner of one of the many railway-bridges which span the streets of London there could be seen a few years ago, from five o'clock every morning until half past eight, a tidily set-out coffee-stall, consisting of a trestle and board, upon which stood two large tin cans, with a small fire of charcoal burning under each so as to keep the coffee boiling during the early hours of the morning when the work-people were thronging into the city on their way to their daily toil...

Pages:84

Childrens   **ISBN:** *1-59462-373-2*   *MSRP $9.95*

My Life and Work
Henry Ford

QTY

Henry Ford revolutionized the world with his implementation of mass production for the Model T automobile. Gain valuable business insight into his life and work with his own auto-biography... "We have only started on our development of our country we have not as yet, with all our talk of wonderful progress, done more than scratch the surface. The progress has been wonderful enough but..."

Pages:300

Biographies/   **ISBN:** *1-59462-198-5*   *MSRP $21.95*

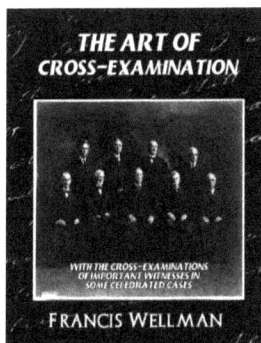

The Art of Cross-Examination
Francis Wellman

QTY

I presume it is the experience of every author, after his first book is published upon an important subject, to be almost overwhelmed with a wealth of ideas and illustrations which could readily have been included in his book, and which to his own mind, at least, seem to make a second edition inevitable. Such certainly was the case with me; and when the first edition had reached its sixth impression in five months, I rejoiced to learn that it seemed to my publishers that the book had met with a sufficiently favorable reception to justify a second and considerably enlarged edition. ...

Reference   ISBN: *1-59462-647-2*

Pages:412

MSRP $19.95

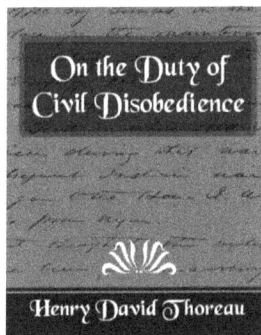

On the Duty of Civil Disobedience
Henry David Thoreau

QTY

Thoreau wrote his famous essay, On the Duty of Civil Disobedience, as a protest against an unjust but popular war and the immoral but popular institution of slave-owning. He did more than write—he declined to pay his taxes, and was hauled off to gaol in consequence. Who can say how much this refusal of his hastened the end of the war and of slavery?

Law   ISBN: *1-59462-747-9*

Pages:48

MSRP $7.45

Dream Psychology Psychoanalysis for Beginners
Sigmund Freud

QTY

Sigmund Freud, born Sigismund Schlomo Freud (May 6, 1856 - September 23, 1939), was a Jewish-Austrian neurologist and psychiatrist who co-founded the psychoanalytic school of psychology. Freud is best known for his theories of the unconscious mind, especially involving the mechanism of repression; his redefinition of sexual desire as mobile and directed towards a wide variety of objects; and his therapeutic techniques, especially his understanding of transference in the therapeutic relationship and the presumed value of dreams as sources of insight into unconscious desires.

Psychology   ISBN: *1-59462-905-6*

Pages:196

MSRP $15.45

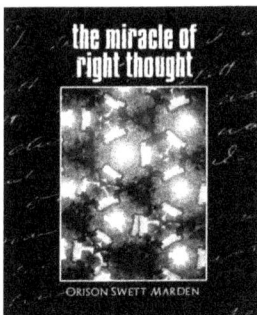

The Miracle of Right Thought
Orison Swett Marden

QTY

Believe with all of your heart that you will do what you were made to do. When the mind has once formed the habit of holding cheerful, happy, prosperous pictures, it will not be easy to form the opposite habit. It does not matter how improbable or how far away this realization may see, or how dark the prospects may be, if we visualize them as best we can, as vividly as possible, hold tenaciously to them and vigorously struggle to attain them, they will gradually become actualized, realized in the life. But a desire, a longing without endeavor, a yearning abandoned or held indifferently will vanish without realization.

Self Help   ISBN: *1-59462-644-8*

Pages:360

MSRP $25.45

The Rosicrucian Cosmo-Conception Mystic Christianity *by Max Heindel*   ISBN: *1-59462-188-8*   **$38.95**
The Rosicrucian Cosmo-conception is not dogmatic, neither does it appeal to any other authority than the reason of the student. It is: not controversial, but is: sent forth in the, hope that it may help to clear...   New Age/Religion Pages 646

Abandonment To Divine Providence *by Jean-Pierre de Caussade*   ISBN: *1-59462-228-0*   **$25.95**
"The Rev. Jean Pierre de Caussade was one of the most remarkable spiritual writers of the Society of Jesus in France in the 18th Century. His death took place at Toulouse in 1751. His works have gone through many editions and have been republished...   Inspirational/Religion Pages 400

Mental Chemistry *by Charles Haanel*   ISBN: *1-59462-192-6*   **$23.95**
Mental Chemistry allows the change of material conditions by combining and appropriately utilizing the power of the mind. Much like applied chemistry creates something new and unique out of careful combinations of chemicals the mastery of mental chemistry...   New Age Pages 354

The Letters of Robert Browning and Elizabeth Barret Barrett 1845-1846 vol II   ISBN: *1-59462-193-4*   **$35.95**
by Robert Browning and Elizabeth Barrett   Biographies Pages 596

Gleanings In Genesis (volume I) *by Arthur W. Pink*   ISBN: *1-59462-130-6*   **$27.45**
Appropriately has Genesis been termed "the seed plot of the Bible" for in it we have, in germ form, almost all of the great doctrines which are afterwards fully developed in the books of Scripture which follow...   Religion/Inspirational Pages 420

The Master Key *by L. W. de Laurence*   ISBN: *1-59462-001-6*   **$30.95**
In no branch of human knowledge has there been a more lively increase of the spirit of research during the past few years than in the study of Psychology, Concentration and Mental Discipline. The requests for authentic lessons in Thought Control, Mental Discipline and...   New Age/Business Pages 422

The Lesser Key Of Solomon Goetia *by L. W. de Laurence*   ISBN: *1-59462-092-X*   **$9.95**
This translation of the first book of the "Lemegton" which is now for the first time made accessible to students of Talismanic Magic was done, after careful collation and edition, from numerous Ancient Manuscripts in Hebrew, Latin, and French...   New Age/Occult Pages 92

Rubaiyat Of Omar Khayyam *by Edward Fitzgerald*   ISBN: *1-59462-332-5*   **$13.95**
Edward Fitzgerald, whom the world has already learned, in spite of his own efforts to remain within the shadow of anonymity, to look upon as one of the rarest poets of the century, was born at Bredfield, in Suffolk, on the 31st of March, 1809. He was the third son of John Purcell...   Music Pages 172

Ancient Law *by Henry Maine*   ISBN: *1-59462-128-4*   **$29.95**
The chief object of the following pages is to indicate some of the earliest ideas of mankind, as they are reflected in Ancient Law, and to point out the relation of those ideas to modern thought.   Religiom/History Pages 452

Far-Away Stories *by William J. Locke*   ISBN: *1-59462-129-2*   **$19.45**
"Good wine needs no bush, but a collection of mixed vintages does. And this book is just such a collection. Some of the stories I do not want to remain buried for ever in the museum files of dead magazine-numbers an author's not unpardonable vanity..."   Fiction Pages 272

Life of David Crockett *by David Crockett*   ISBN: *1-59462-250-7*   **$27.45**
"Colonel David Crockett was one of the most remarkable men of the times in which he lived. Born in humble life, but gifted with a strong will, an indomitable courage, and unremitting perseverance...   Biographies/New Age Pages 424

Lip-Reading *by Edward Nitchie*   ISBN: *1-59462-206-X*   **$25.95**
Edward B. Nitchie, founder of the New York School for the Hard of Hearing, now the Nitchie School of Lip-Reading, Inc, wrote "LIP-READING Principles and Practice". The development and perfecting of this meritorious work on lip-reading was an undertaking...   How-to Pages 400

A Handbook of Suggestive Therapeutics, Applied Hypnotism, Psychic Science   ISBN: *1-59462-214-0*   **$24.95**
by Henry Munro   Health/New Age/Health/Self-help Pages 376

A Doll's House: and Two Other Plays *by Henrik Ibsen*   ISBN: *1-59462-112-8*   **$19.95**
Henrik Ibsen created this classic when in revolutionary 1848 Rome. Introducing some striking concepts in playwriting for the realist genre, this play has been studied the world over.   Fiction/Classics/Plays 308

The Light of Asia *by sir Edwin Arnold*   ISBN: *1-59462-204-3*   **$13.95**
In this poetic masterpiece, Edwin Arnold describes the life and teachings of Buddha. The man who was to become known as Buddha to the world was born as Prince Gautama of India but he rejected the worldly riches and abandoned the reigns of power when...   Religion/History/Biographies Pages 170

The Complete Works of Guy de Maupassant *by Guy de Maupassant*   ISBN: *1-59462-157-8*   **$16.95**
"For days and days, nights and nights, I had dreamed of that first kiss which was to consecrate our engagement, and I knew not on what spot I should put my lips..."   Fiction/Classics Pages 240

The Art of Cross-Examination *by Francis L. Wellman*   ISBN: *1-59462-309-0*   **$26.95**
Written by a renowned trial lawyer, Wellman imparts his experience and uses case studies to explain how to use psychology to extract desired information through questioning.   How-to/Science/Reference Pages 408

Answered or Unanswered? *by Louisa Vaughan*   ISBN: *1-59462-248-5*   **$10.95**
Miracles of Faith in China   Religion Pages 112

The Edinburgh Lectures on Mental Science (1909) *by Thomas*   ISBN: *1-59462-008-3*   **$11.95**
This book contains the substance of a course of lectures recently given by the writer in the Queen Street Hall, Edinburgh. Its purpose is to indicate the Natural Principles governing the relation between Mental Action and Material Conditions...   New Age/Psychology Pages 148

Ayesha *by H. Rider Haggard*   ISBN: *1-59462-301-5*   **$24.95**
Verily and indeed it is the unexpected that happens! Probably if there was one person upon the earth from whom the Editor of this, and of a certain previous history, did not expect to hear again...   Classics Pages 380

Ayala's Angel *by Anthony Trollope*   ISBN: *1-59462-352-X*   **$29.95**
The two girls were both pretty, but Lucy who was twenty-one who supposed to be simple and comparatively unattractive, whereas Ayala was credited, as her Bombwhat romantic name might show, with poetic charm and a taste for romance. Ayala when her father died was nineteen...   Fiction Pages 484

The American Commonwealth *by James Bryce*   ISBN: *1-59462-286-8*   **$34.45**
An interpretation of American democratic political theory. It examines political mechanics and society from the perspective of Scotsman James Bryce   Politics Pages 572

Stories of the Pilgrims *by Margaret P. Pumphrey*   ISBN: *1-59462-116-0*   **$17.95**
This book explores pilgrims religious oppression in England as well as their escape to Holland and eventual crossing to America on the Mayflower, and their early days in New England...   History Pages 268